# Divine Intervention:

## One Woman's Journey Through The Storms Of Life

By

## CARLINE EDOUARD

First paperback edition: March 2021

ISBN-13: 978-1-7364929-0-1

# ACKNOWLEDGEMENTS

I want to thank God most of all, because without Him I truly have no idea where I would be. In Him, I live and move and have my beings.

I'm eternally grateful to my parents, Mrs. Claudiane Edouard and Mr. Winston Edouard. They taught me discipline, love, manners, respect, and so much more that has helped me succeed in life.

Special thanks to my boys Gecarr G. Pierre and Isaiah G. Pierre, my joy and my pride! You guys make both the journey and destination worthwhile and I would do it all over again just to have you here in this lifetime with me. You keep me going even when I don't feel like it. You make me choose life over and over and over again. I love you to pieces!!!

I owe an enormous debt of gratitude to Dr. Roger Argelio Alvarez, DO, MPH: You went above and beyond to make sure that I was both alive and well. Everyday before you left work— whether in your clinic next door or in the hospital (UMH)— you always came to my room to say hi and to reassure me that everything was going to be okay. You stayed late when you could have been having dinner with your family, but you stayed just to make sure I got the proper care I needed. One day you came to see me and you realized I had difficulties breathing because of a fluid build up in my abdomen. You stayed past your scheduled shift and you did a paracentesis (an abdominal tap) to remove the ascites. After the procedure, I was able to breathe and I slept like a baby. I thank God for you!

To my Cardiac surgeon Dr. Joseph Lamelas: MD: you are the absolute best in South Florida. Thank you so much for the difference you made in my life and being so skilled at what you do!

I'm also immensely grateful to the University of Miami Hospital staff and all the wonderful nurses who took care of me and those of you who risked your job and prayed with me, you guys are awesome!!!

I want to thank all the doctors, nurses and staff at Jackson Hospital. A very special thanks to those of you that took care of me. I am forever grateful!

Emory Hospital and staff, thank you for taking care of me and baby Isaiah!

Zion Hospital and staff, thank you for taking care of me and baby Gecarr!

I want to acknowledge Pastor Marie Fernande Constant, Baptist Church Of The Living God (L'Eglise

Baptiste Du Dieu Vivant), the staff and members. I can't thank you enough for your prayers.

A very special thanks to my friend Nadine Budzynski for being closer than a sister. Thank you for always being the person I could turn to during those dark and desperate times. I love you and I am grateful for your counsel, thoughts and prayers. Thank you to your daddy (Papa Jacques), the church in Paris, and your husband (Kenneth) for their prayers.

A special thanks to Bishop Marc Guillaume and your precious wife Elmire Guillaume for your words of encouragement and your prayers. You are more than friends, you are family!

To my family & friends: My siblings, I love you all! My nieces and nephews, (auntie) love you! Carlmax Costume & Family. I appreciate you all!

Writing a book about your life is a surreal process. I'm forever indebted to Cheyanne for her editorial help, keen insight, and ongoing support in bringing my stories to life. It's because of your efforts and encouragement that I have a legacy to pass on to my family where one didn't exist before.

# Divine Intervention:

## One Woman's Journey Through The Storms Of Life

Dear Sis Sherley,
Wishing you a Therapeutic Joy
while reading this book !!

with love,
Carline Edouard

# Table of Contents

## THERE WILL BE BURDENS

In my life, I've seen my fair share of struggles. I know what it's like to kiss someone goodbye and not know if you'll ever see them again. I've lived with uncertainty and heartbreak. I know what it's like to wonder if I'll wake up in the morning…to wonder if *today* is my *last* day. I've thought the worst about myself and others. Yet through all of that, I've come to deeply understand one fundamental truth: God created us to conquer the storms of life; not to be conquered by them.

After years of facing life's tsunamis, tidal waves, hurricanes, typhoons, and cyclones, I realized something pivotal. I realized that God never promised us smooth sailing. In fact, Jesus himself warns us that we will face hardships. He tells us that in his word that, "In this world, you will have trouble. But take heart! I have overcome the world." (John 16:33)

Jesus acknowledges and prepares us for the storms of life. Not only does he remind us that they will happen, but he also offers us a beacon of hope. Do not be dismayed by your trials and suffering. *Don't* for one moment, believe the lies of the enemy; God has not forsaken you. Fix your gaze on the Lord, and find your peace amid the fear, pain, and uncertainty.

Let your heart be reminded that God created you to conquer the storm, not be defeated by it. He will never send you more challenges than you can bear. There have been so many times when I've thought that I couldn't go on with life any longer. I would cry out to the Lord to help me because I didn't know if I was strong enough to withstand the ferocity of my circumstances, but God knew differently. He knew the strength that was within me, the strength that I wasn't even aware of. Only He knows the depths of the courage that reside within you.

Your circumstances do not define how strong you are. They only serve as a means to show you what lies within yourself. God only burdens a person with those circumstances, which at that moment in their lives, are most useful for their development. Your experience is merely a place for spiritualization. God is using this as a means to grow you into the person who you were always called to be. The spiritual growing process can be painful, but during our pain, God has made it clear to us that he will not forsake us.

God gives us evidence of His promise over and over again in the Bible. In Matthew 14:22-33, God gives us the perfect illustration through the actions of his disciple, Peter. Peter is surrounded by crashing waves amid a relentless storm, but he is not alone. Jesus walks through the storm toward Peter. Jesus doesn't leave his disciples alone, helpless and powerless to do anything to help prevent Peter from drowning into the depths below. Jesus leaves the shore and meets them in the midst of it all.

In the book of Jonah, God provides for his prophet Jonah even as he actively defies God's command. Jonah finds himself face to face with the consequences of his own stubbornness.

When he is tossed into the sea, the Lord could have sent a different creature to punish Jonah for his disobedience. Instead, He sent a large fish that could safely ingest Jonah without hurting him. God continued not only to use Jonah to complete His will, but also provided for him by keeping him safe while he was preaching in Nineveh.

Like Job, I have learned through the hard life lessons that we cannot change our circumstances. They are sent to us: to test us, to grow us, and to bring us closer to God. I now accept that the best thing for me is to listen to what He says. I am who God says I am, where He says I'm supposed to be, and I will be where He says I need to be. On the good days I accept it with gratitude and a smile. On the bad days I accept it with resistance and patience. I try to understand what God is saying to me. What am I supposed to learn during this storm? What direction should I be going? At the end of the day, I am not in control. This realization doesn't make me absolutely happy, but I have a clear horizon opening in front of me, free from the rainy curtains and filled with the sunny light of awareness.

# CHAPTER 1

## *More than a Statistic*

My life has been far from ordinary. Some might say that growing up as a young Haitian/Dominican girl to believer parents destined me to live a life far beyond the reaches of ordinary.

I grew up under the hot sun that kissed *Hispaniola* on the Haitian side of the island. Our brightly colored home was always overflowing with love and laughter. To this day, I can still hear the echoes of my family's laughter and smell the welcoming aroma of fresh corossol, kenèp, and oranges… even if I close my eyes. The mere thought of it brings me back to my childhood home, and makes me smile.

In the 80s, Haiti was a safe and friendly place, and it was my little slice of heaven. The buildings themselves reflected the tropical paradise that grew around the trees and shrubs. The houses are tall and brightly painted with an array of colors. They are works of art that display the brightest of tones. And the cars...the cars were just as bright and beautiful as the houses that lined Haiti's roads. The first nine years of my life were blessed by the rich traditions and beautiful Haitian culture, but it was also peppered with a struggle that began before I was even born; a struggle that has stayed with me every day of my life.

My father never wanted to have girls. He thought they were precocious, and he was afraid to have a daughter because he thought that he might not be in our lives long enough to protect us. If he had a girl, who would protect her if he couldn't? But that's how he felt before I was born. It wasn't long before he changed his mind. Even now, he'll brag, "that without you, I never would have changed my mind. I believed that raising a daughter would always be a handful." He never imagined himself enjoying the tears of turbulent emotions, navigating the unpredictable up and down moods of a teen girl or having to learn to cope with the idea of his little girl falling in love. Instead, he was more than content to only have sons. He enjoyed the rough and tumble action that came with raising boys. When each of my three older brothers were born, he was thrilled. He rejoiced in all their shenanigans and adventures. Every strange and wriggling creature my brothers brought back home was a treasure…every wrestling match that almost pulled his back out was a welcome delight. Life with a household of boys was bliss for my father. Then the unimaginable happened. My older brother, Alexandre (who was just an infant at the time), unexpectedly passed away. His death caused my parents to question everything. They wondered if God had a different plan for them and their children— one that they had never imagined.

With the loss of Alexandre and his memory forever in their hearts and these new questions about God's will in their minds, my parents began to pray. They asked God for direction and for clarity about the path He wanted them to walk. My brother's death was the catalyst for change in my father's heart. Not only did it strengthen the relationship he had with God, but it also created a new desire for him…the desire to have a daughter.

When my father finally admitted to my mother that he would like to have a daughter, she was thrilled. Even though each of her little boys held a special place in her heart, my mother had always hoped she would have a daughter.

Together, my parents began praying for another child. And this time, even my father prayed for a girl.

When my mother had missed her period for two months, she knew beyond a doubt that she was pregnant. As my father and mother celebrated God's goodness for blessing them with another child, the thought that my mother's pregnancy would be anything but ordinary didn't even cross their minds. They had already experienced the joys of three normal and healthy pregnancies…why would this one be any different? However, my mother's first prenatal visit proved to be far from ordinary, blissful experience they had in the past. My parents were eager to hear my heartbeat and take their first peek at me on the ultrasound, but when the doctor went to find me safe and snug in my mother's womb, I wasn't there. Both my parents and the doctor were shocked. Everyone had questions. The doctor wondered if my mother was really pregnant; my mother wondered if she had unknowingly had a miscarriage; and my father wondered where God was in the midst of yet another potential tragedy.

On their way home, my parents discussed what they should do moving forward. They knew their options were limited: they could wait and see if my mother got her period, run multiple tests on my mother to ensure that she didn't have any illness that could be causing her to miss cycles, or they could stand firm in their faith that she was pregnant and get another opinion. It took all of my parent's courage to choose faith as the option in the face of a bizarre unknown. My father trusted my mother's intuition. My mother knew that she was pregnant, and she also knew that God would not have told her she was pregnant if she wasn't.

My mother and father searched for a secondary opinion over the course of the next month. Each time they found a new physician, the doctor would say there was no need to do anything more if the pregnancy test was positive. By the time they were able to find a doctor who could locate me on the ultrasound, my mother was sure she'd already been pregnant for three months. When she told the doctor so, he informed my parents that my mother had something called Repressed Pregnancy, or as my parents knew it, Pèdisyon.

Pèdisyon (also known as *Perdition*) is a Haitian biomedical syndrome where a woman carries a fetus for longer than the usual prenatal term. A woman can be pregnant for as long as several months or several years without having the baby show up on an ultrasound. Among the Haitian people, it is a common health problem, and it is believed that the baby is held in the womb by a Voodoo Priest using magical forces. When my parents finally learned the strange situation surrounding my creation, they knew that God had destined me to be a fighter. They knew that it was His divine plan for me to enter into the world and take it by storm. After three months of being held in my mother's womb, unable to grow and mature, God released me. My mother was able to carry me normally. My parents were still afraid for me, and they had every right to be, but God's grace already guarded my life. During her pregnancy, my mother had to be closely monitored. Even though the Repressed Pregnancy caused her to carry me for twelve long months, I was safely delivered into the world.

Some people might think that this should have been the moment that God allowed us to rest from our string of trials and tribulations…but God was not finished growing my family yet. During what should have been a joyous time of celebration for my parents and a time of acclimation and family bonding, I became sick. I'm not sure if my poor health as an infant was a sign from God of what was to come, but with full confidence, I believe that if it were not for the strength and endurance my mother passed on to me as she handled her Pèdisyon, I might not be here today.

When I turned one, my father knew that God was calling him to do something drastic for the sake of my life and my health. After talking to friends, neighbors, and doctors, he decided that the best place for me to receive the medical care I needed would be the United States. Even though it broke my parent's hearts to leave our home in Haiti, my father insisted that this would be the best decision for our family. Leaning on God's provision, my father moved to the US by himself, leaving us behind in our colorful home. He planned on filing for the entire family's citizenship while in America, filling out form after form, explaining that we were from Haiti and stating the reason why we wanted to immigrate. The plan was that after our files were approved, we would leave the island and fly over to meet him. However, God had other plans.

Somehow the paperwork for myself, my mother, and my siblings was delayed. We were forced to stay in Haiti while he anxiously worked and faithfully prayed for us miles away in America. Neither of my parents were confident in my ability to continue living a happy, healthy childhood in Haiti, but against the odds, I not only did grow up, but I led a relatively normal childhood. I was a cheerful child, always ready for anything with a smile. I worked hard in school, and my grades reflected just how intelligent I was.

I was friendly, but I kept to myself. I was a very reserved kid. I never had a lot of friends. I was very quiet, and very laid back. To this day, I would still consider myself an observer. More so as a kid, but I still see the impact it has on my life even as an adult. I'm still an introvert, and ever since childhood, I built walls around myself. I didn't open up to people. I kept my life private, and I remained socially isolated. These were all self-protective measures in an effort to keep myself from getting hurt. But on the outside? On the outside I was smiling Carline, and no one ever saw me unhappy.

My parents worked hard to provide for both myself and my five siblings. We didn't want for anything. I'm sure there were some luxuries we didn't get a chance to experience, but looking back on it now, all I can remember is having a full stomach, a warm bed, and a roof over my head. My house was always full of laughter, and my heart was full of love. Life was simple and carefree. I couldn't have asked for more.

Even though my father had left for America not long before I turned one, I didn't even know that he left. I didn't realize my father was gone because my *grandpa* (Massillon, my father's father) was always around. I really thought he was my dad, both me and my younger brother were convinced because Grandpa Massillon was the prominent male figure in our life. Eventually, my Aunt Imose (my mother's little sister) sat me and my younger brother down. She grabbed the picture album off the shelf and opened the cover. She asked me to point out my father. I did as I was told, and pointed to Grandpa Massillon.

"My dad?" I asked. "Massillon is my dad."

"No, Carline." my Aunt said, shaking her head. "No. Grandpa is your dad's dad...*not yours.*"

"What?" I asked, thinking she was playing a trick on me.

Imose flipped through a few more pages in the album, landing on a picture of Winston, my father. She tapped her finger against the page, saying, "This is your father! He is in America!"

The women in my family worked. Really worked. My mother worked both as a nurse and a seamstress. She was a sort of fashion designer. She used to make all kinds of wedding dresses and gowns. There was constantly a half-sewn dress on her lap and an assortment of mixed fabrics on her knee. When she wasn't looking, I'd sneak off with a piece of fabric and use it to make dresses and clothes for my dolls. As it turns out, the fabric wasn't extra, and it was actually intended to be the right or left sleeve of a client's dress.

"CARLIIIIIIINE!"

She was not happy with my creativity, but that didn't stop me. I would entertain myself by making "products." I'd sneak into my mother's bedroom and mix together her lotions and face creams. I'd water them down and try to make sweet smelling perfumes. I'd add soap and water into the lotion bottles and shake them up. I liked watching all the different solutions mix together. Colors would evolve, and I loved it. At night, my mother would come back to bed and try to put on her lotions, but it wouldn't take long for her to realize that her lotions were ruined. One time, I mixed baby powder in with her hair relaxer. She went to put it on and—

"CARLIIIIIIINE!"

My aunt was a caterer, and that made her a busy woman. She catered and she made wedding cakes. They were always working, my mother and my aunt, while us kids ran around the house. We'd weave back and forth between them, laughing and screaming as we went. I don't know how they ever got any work done, but they did.

I always think of my mother as a fashion designer, but we had daily reminders of her expertise in the medical field. Every morning, my mother would line us all up— during flu season (or in the summer before fall term)— and vaccinate us. But for most mornings— everyone from my brothers to my cousins would stand in a straight line as my mother dispersed our daily doses of tea. We all hated it with a passion. And while the older kids were given their tea to drink at their leisure (I found out later that they were paying the maids to drink their portion for them), I, along with the rest of the little kids, had to stand in line and drink every last drop in front of my mother. We weren't allowed to leave until we'd finished the entire cup…and it was bitter. It was *so* bitter. Somehow, we managed, but if I close my eyes, I can still taste that horrible, pungent tea.

Saturday was always a party in my house. We'd do all our favorite things. We'd play music and eat and just have fun with family. As far as hanging out at someone else's house… we weren't allowed to do that. My mother never let us go over to friend's houses. I'm not sure why. Maybe that's why I'm so reserved, come to think of it. Lots of people would come over to our house, you know, like family, and our cousins and stuff. My family was very caring, they just loved people in general. We'd laugh and tell jokes and sing. We always had a good time.

It wasn't all fun and games. I wish I could say that I miss my childhood, but it was a struggle. My health made a lot of things difficult for me. I was a happy go lucky child, but it was a terse balance.

It was hard for me and my family to cope. Honestly, it's something I still struggle with…wondering why my brothers and the rest of the world get to be healthy. Why am I the one who struggles just to breathe?

# CHAPTER 2

## *Needing Answers*

My life completely changed the year I turned nine. I went from a young girl full of life to a girl who had to accept the real possibility that I might never see my tenth birthday. The day that my whole life changed started out like any other day. The sun was shining, I had things that I wanted to accomplish for the day, and I couldn't think of a single thing that could stop me from making the most out of the day. Just as quickly as a flash flood, the breath was stolen from my lungs. I'd never had difficulty breathing before. I immediately knew something very wrong was happening. I remember fighting back tears and panic as I tried to force myself to take deep, even breaths…but nothing can convince your brain that your body isn't suffocating when you can't take a normal breath. It felt like I was drowning. My body was overwhelmed, the weight of my chest caving in and crushing my lungs was too much to endure. It was like a massive stack of bricks had been dropped on my chest. Every day it felt like my own body was trying to kill me.

The pain was indescribable. It was a constant, relentless, and aggressive ache from deep within me. There were so many times when I was gasping for breath that I would clutch my chest and cry. My mother held me, and tried to comfort me. I was terrified, and even in my panic, I knew my parents were, too. They didn't know what was wrong with me, and no matter how many doctors we saw, no one could give us the answers we so desperately needed. I was poked, prodded, and examined more times than I could count. My arms began to feel like pincushions from countless blood tests and pinpricks that were supposed to determine what was making me sick, but nothing worked. What was wrong with me?

When test after test came back negative, the doctors stopped trying to figure out what the root cause was, and instead tried to focus on making me more comfortable. They worked in vain to treat the symptoms…as if treating my symptoms would somehow end the source of all my suffering. I was prescribed pills, tonics, offered obscure home remedies, vitamins, and anything else under the sun the doctors could think of. Still, nothing worked. I couldn't breathe, and with every failed attempt to heal me, my condition worsened. My parents knew that if they couldn't find an answer soon, it was likely that I would not live much longer.

Looking back, I know now that it was God's divine intervention that led me and my mother to the waiting room of *Medicine Intern Hospital*. I was unsure of what to expect during the visit. I was nervous, yet hopeful.

*Would this doctor actually know what was happening to my body? How would they succeed where others had failed?*

As soon as he entered the room, the examination felt different. Unlike the other doctors, Dr. Paul Henry Morisset listened carefully to everything my mother told him about my condition. He nodded, and scribbled a few notes down on my chart. Then he told me to open my mouth wide. He looked into the far corners of my mouth and rubbed the back of my throat with a cotton swab.

"Do you have a family history of heart disease?" Dr. Morisset asked.

My mother shook her head.

"Has Carline ever come down with a high fever that lasted an exceptionally long time?"

My mother shook her head again.

*What did my heart have to do with my throat?*

15

I remember being confused by his questions, but as my mother explained our family history, I could see the gears turning in Dr. Morisset's head. He quickly ordered an electrocardiogram and an echocardiogram. He explained that these tests would look at my heart and its functions, and would work in conjunction with a fresh set of blood tests.

From that point on, it felt like everything was happening in slow motion. It felt so strange…knowing that we were *finally* so close to finding out what was happening.

When the results of the test came back, Dr. Morisset paused, looking back and forth between my file and my mother and me. He paused, and took a long time to speak. His look said it all, and even at nine years old, I knew it meant that whatever words were about to follow would shatter my world forever. He took a deep breath, and set my charts down on the counter next to him. He looked at my mother and told her that I had RHD.

"RHD?" she asked.

The doctor nodded.

"RHD is short for Rheumatic Heart Disease…RHD. It's a rare heart condition."

I looked at my mother for some kind of explanation. Before we could ask anything else, he went on to say just what RHD was going to do to me.

*Carline, age six, at her home in Haiti*

"It causes permanent damage to the heart valves. The condition typically originates after a spike in an extremely high fever. This usually happens during a strep infection or a case of Scarlet fever that is either left untreated, or is under-treated. While the degree of deterioration in the heart valves differs from person to person…it is likely that your valves are so destroyed…"

He kept pausing, and I knew that was bad.

"In Carline's case…it's highly probable that there will not be a long life time expectancy."

# CHAPTER 3

## *Racing Thoughts*

My mother thanked Doctor Morisset, and we left the hospital. Time was still moving slowly for me. I didn't understand everything that the doctor had said to my mother, but I did understand one thing; I was going to die.

I was filled with fear on the way home from the hospital. It was quiet, and neither I nor my mother said anything. The night was dark and a little chilly. It was the kind of night that I would usually love, but not that night. Instead of watching the bright colored cars race by, or looking up at the trees that swayed in the wind, I was consumed with the many questions that raced through my mind.

*What did it all mean? I'm just a child. I barely started my life and now some doctor is telling me that it is all going to end? I'm not ready to die.*

The days that followed felt like I was walking around in a haze. With each breath I struggled to take, I thought I was one breath closer to death. How do you make amends with death as a child? I sure didn't know how. I tried ignoring the inevitable. I would use anything I could to distract me: my brothers, school, the little bits of cloth I used to make doll dresses…but my thoughts always returned to dying.

*Would dying hurt? Would I see a bright light at the end of the tunnel? Would I meet Jesus?*

I wasn't sure who I could talk to about the many thoughts that flew through my mind. Whenever I talked to my parents about how scared I was, they would assure me that they were going to pray for a miracle. Their faith was stronger than mine. While I wanted to believe that God would deliver me from my disease, that I would have a miraculous healing overnight, and that I would soon be a normal kid like my brothers, I had doubts. My symptoms progressively got worse, and even more doubts and fears followed. I doubted that God would show up to heal my small body. Perhaps He had more important things to do. Why would He heal someone as small as me when there were so many other people in the world who needed help? My parents would tell me stories of God's healing powers from the Bible, but still, fear prevailed. Just because it had happened to the centenarian's daughter, didn't mean that the Lord would heal me, too.

I wanted to put my trust in a medical miracle. The doctors tried so many different methods, that I thought surely one of these would deliver me from death's doorstep. Something would help me. There had to be something they were missing. There had to be some kind of cure out there that would fix everything. But nothing did.

It didn't take long before the doctors gave up. The team of doctors who were responsible for finding a treatment for a case as severe as mine eventually informed my mother that 'it was too late for me.' They told us there was no hope of a cure. They encouraged my parents to treasure the time we still had together before I would die. When friends and family would come visit, they would also encourage my mother to let me go. They'd speak about my condition, which grew into hushed whispers when they thought I was in the room.

"There isn't any point in trying to hold on," they would say. "it's just her time."

Both my parents told me that God had a plan for me, but I'll admit that His plan was far beyond my understanding. Each day they would get on their knees and pray for my healing, yet each day I would only get worse. I began to wonder how a God who sent His only son to die on the cross for me could let me suffer like this. What was His plan? Did He really provide for me this whole time, only to let me die now? Little did I realize just how significantly God was planning to move in my life. I couldn't see His hand in the midst of my storm, but He was ever-present, walking beside me every step of the way.

# CHAPTER 4

## *A Child's Vigil*

It was late in the year, nearly Fall, and hope seemed completely unattainable. Right as I was giving up on life and accepting the fact that it was God's plan for me to die young, my father got the call he'd been waiting on for so long: our paperwork was processed, and our Green Cards had been approved.

We could come to the United States.

Finally, after so many days and nights of pain and sorrow, my family and I cried tears of joy. There was no place in Haiti where the surgeons could successfully perform an open-heart surgery, but the US was well known for several hospitals that could perform the operation I needed, despite the level of deterioration my heart was at. At last, I began to hope.

My emotions washed over me like waves. In the course of several hours, I went from experiencing relief that I might not die, to fearing that the surgery wouldn't work, and was eventually hit with the realization that I would have to leave my home. The thought of leaving my island filled me with such anxiety. For all that Haiti wasn't, it was everything that I loved. I would miss the smells, sights, and the people.

*Would America have a Christmas midnight supper? Would the people there believe in Liberté, Egalité, Fraternité?*

As I watched my family pack all of our belongings, I wondered if leaving Haiti meant seeing my last brightly colored *Tatap* Bus and taking my last sips of tasse de thé. Our departure would mean closing this chapter of my life. It was a lot to process for me, moving and surgery and leaving everything and everyone I'd ever known and loved. I wasn't sure what awaited me when we would turn the page and start the next chapter, but I knew that God would be with me and my family just as He had always been.

For the first time in years, I was going to see my father. When he left Haiti for the first time so many years ago, he'd sailed a boat up to the coast of Florida. But this time, he flew back to the island to escort my mother, my brothers, and me back to the United States. After being gone for so long, he was given a warm welcome back to Haiti. Even though my father had returned, I wouldn't see much of him until after my surgery.

The day after my father returned, my mother and my younger brother and I went to the airport. I'd said goodbye to my older brothers, who were going to join us in America later. It was hard to say goodbye, but I knew they'd be with us again soon. While I'd seen airplanes before, this was the first time I'd ever been on one. We boarded the plane and sat near the back of the cabin. Now a-days, it isn't likely that someone with a serious heart condition like mine would take a commercial flight, but I did. I slept most of the way there. It was a long flight, and all I can really remember about it is being sick. So many of my memories from childhood are shrouded in illness, that I don't remember the finite details and that came so easily to my brothers.

My parents had already been in touch with various American doctors, so as soon as we landed in Florida at the *Miami International Airport*, an ambulance was already waiting for us at the curbside. I was rushed off the plane and hurriedly escorted to the ambulance. It was my first ambulance ride. I put my head on the gurney and laid back. I listened to the siren screaming our urgent need for the hospital, and it made my head swim. I didn't know what was going to happen next. It was all happening so quickly that I barely had time to process all of my emotions. I was rushed to *Jackson Memorial Hospital* and immediately admitted to their pediatric wing. As the doctors ran their never-ending tests and reviewed my labs, they explained that they had hoped they could treat my heart defect without surgery. My stomach instantly filled with butterflies and hope.

I hoped I wouldn't need surgery; not then, not ever. Once again, however, God had other plans. When my results came back, the doctors discovered that it was too late. My valve was far too collapsed for any treatment other than surgery. They had no choice other than operating. I needed to have an emergency *Mitral Valve Replacement Open-heart surgery* as fast as possible because my valve was extremely clotted. That's when I learned that heart disease does not discriminate. It will take the lives of those both young and old. No one is immune to the destruction it creates in your body.

They scheduled my surgery 'first thing in the morning,' and I was riddled with fear the entire night. I clutched my hands together and fervently prayed to the Lord for strength and peace. Almost instantly, an otherworldly calmness settled over me like a blanket. I knew, no matter what happened, I was going to be okay. God was in control. To this day, I still believe that God sent an angel to stay with me that night. He gave me comfort while I slept, and in the morning, my angel followed me to surgery. I vividly remember a man walking alongside me and reciting Psalms 91 as the nurses wheeled me into the operating room. These verses echoed through my heart and mind as the darkness closed in around me before my surgery.

*"He that dwelleth in the secret place of the most High shall abide under the shadow of the Almighty.*

*I will say of the LORD, He is my refuge and my fortress: my God; in Him will I trust.*

*Surely He shall deliver thee from the snare of the fowler, and from the noisome pestilence.*

*He shall cover thee with His feathers, and under His wings shalt thou trust: His truth shall be thy shield and buckler.*

*Thou shalt not be afraid for the terror by night; nor for the arrow that flieth by day;*

*Nor for the pestilence that walketh in darkness; nor for the destruction that wasteth at noonday.*

*A thousand shall fall at thy side, and ten thousand at thy right hand; but it shall not come nigh thee.*

*Only with thine eyes shalt thou behold and see the reward of the wicked.*

*Because thou hast made the LORD, which is my refuge, even the most High, thy habitation;*

*There shall no evil befall thee, neither shall any plague come nigh thy dwelling.*

*For He shall give His angels charge over thee, to keep thee in all thy ways.*

*They shall bear thee up in their hands, lest thou dash thy foot against a stone.*

*Thou shalt tread upon the lion and adder: the young lion and the dragon shalt thou trample under feet.*

*Because he hath set his love upon me, therefore will I deliver him: I will set him on high, because he hath known my name.*

*He shall call upon me, and I will answer him: I will be with him in trouble; I will deliver him, and honour him.*

*With long life will I satisfy him, and shew him my salvation."*

*Psalms 91 (KJV)*

# CHAPTER 5

## *The Table*

*Light....*

That was the first thing that made me realize my
surgery had been a success...light. The sterile, bright light of
the hospital shone through my closed eyelids, warming my
eyes. The sound of the beeping monitors, and the sense of
being rolled down a hallway...these were the next things that
hit me. I couldn't tell which direction I was going, and I had
no way of knowing. It was as if I'd lost all connection with
my body. I could have been lying down or on the floor of a
car and I wouldn't have known the difference. I couldn't
speak to the "driver" or ask for directions or the results of my
surgery. I was forced to be the silent passenger. It was
disorienting— being aware of my senses but being unable to
use them to move or speak.

I could hear people around me talking, discussing how well my *Mechanical Mitral Valve Replacement* surgery went. I didn't know if they were doctors or family. My brain felt foggy, and my eyes, arms, and legs felt like they were strapped down to the table, although I knew they weren't. I couldn't even twitch a finger to let anyone know I was alive.

I couldn't move, I couldn't scream, and I couldn't open my eyes. It still felt like I was in my own body but not in control of it.

*They were wrong*, I thought to myself. *The surgery wasn't a success…I'm dead.*

It wasn't until a few hours later that I was able to open my eyes and see the tiny tubes and wires attached to my body. I felt like a science experiment that was on the verge of going disastrously wrong, needles prodding my skin and medical tools surrounding me on every side. I was Frankenstein's monster, suffocating in medical advancement. But there was another part of me— the bravest part, I believe— that recognized what was happening. I was *alive*. True, I was weak, cold, and confused…but feeling all of those things… being able to sense the objects touching me— meant that I was alive.

I spent two months recovering. November came and went, and I found myself sitting in the Pediatric Wing of *Jackson Memorial Hospital* for Christmas. At first, I was devastated to miss my first Christmas in America. I wanted to go to an American church service and see the Christmas lights decorated on palm trees! I wanted to fantasize about the parts of this vast new county that actually got snow. I wanted to spend it with my family, blending new traditions with old ones. When I was told that I wasn't going to be discharged in time for Christmas, I expected to spend my time uneventfully in bed, pining over all of the things that could have been. But the time in the hospital was almost made up for when something I never could have imagined took place. The *Miami Heat* basketball team visited the hospital! The local paper, the *Miami Herald Newspaper*, came along with the team, snapped pictures and interviewed myself, my parents, and the other children. They asked questions about who our favorite player was, and if we were excited to meet them. They handed out presents and autographs and merchandise, and every child in that room looked like they were so happy they could burst; it was unrecognizable as the grimly labeled 'critical cases' we were usually referred to as.

In the pictures, my grin reaches ear to ear. Every time I look at the photos, it reminds me that it was just another way that God was looking out for me. I needed the ray of sunshine their visit brought. It was a breath of fresh air. It had been a long time since I could inhale deeply enough to enjoy something so sweet. Their visit was all I could talk about for days afterward. I would replay what happened over and over again with anyone who would take the time to listen.

When the surprise of their visit wore off, I passed the time by watching TV, reading, journaling, crafting, and playing cards. I never shied away from trying new activities. I had all the time in the world, so why not try it all? While I did sometimes play with the other children in the wing, I spent a lot of time on private activities and things to keep me busy. It wasn't that I didn't want to make friends while I was in the hospital, but there was a language barrier. The hospital had translators on hand, but there's only so much translating you can handle at a time. I didn't speak a word of English, and my head was already stuffed full of so much French and Creole (and what little left over Spanish had hung around from my earliest years with my father's Dominican side of the family while I was still in Haiti) that I didn't have the time or the energy to learn English while I was in the hospital.

I did make friends with a girl who attended a local church. Somehow the conversation came up, and I don't remember if it was me or my mother who had actually spoken to her about it, but my mother started talking to a few of the other church members that came to visit the young girl who happened to be my roommate. After my mother found out more information, she started going to the Sunday services. She is still a member of that church to this day. It was another reminder that God puts the right people in your life at the right time.

When I wasn't playing cards or watching TV, I was working on physical therapy exercises. The goal of these exercises was to try and regain strength and balance. The exercises always seemed simple at first glance, but in my weakened condition, they were exhausting. I struggled the most with regaining my balance and having enough stamina left over to complete simple activities. It took such a long time after my daily PT (Physical Therapy) to have enough strength to resume basic tasks. I was nothing like the playful, energetic girl I had been three short years ago.

At first, I was frustrated with my progress. I wanted to be back to normal immediately, but I knew I had to compromise with myself. I would rest while I was in the hospital, regain my strength, and then when I went home I would be able to push myself until I had all of my old strength and stamina back. With this in mind, the days dragged on ever so slowly until I could finally go home. When they did release me, they told my parents I needed to be put on (what was then referred to as) the Cardiac diet.

The Cardiac diet was a strict one, and it was far different than the spicy Creole food I was used to eating. With the doctor's strict instructions, I was only allowed to eat fruits, vegetables, and foods rich in fibers and Omega-3 fatty acids. Even though we still ate really healthy, my parents had to adjust their cooking to include plenty of whole grains, lean poultry, and fish. They were also told that they had to be sure to exclude things that were high in salt and sugar— all the normal and tasty foods that other children my age were able to consume. Still, I couldn't complain. If this was the price I had to pay to stay alive and healthy, I would gladly forfeit my right to eat everything salty and sugary. I certainly had been through far worse than a strict diet.

I left the hospital in a wheelchair, and it embarrassed me to no end. I struggled and fought and argued and pleaded with the doctors to leave the hospital's sliding double doors in crutches. I could learn to be okay with crutches, but I could *not* learn to be okay with a wheelchair.

"Please don't make me use this. I don't need it. I really don't."

Then I would have to wait for the translator to take the French or Creole sentences I'd said, translate them into English, get the doctor's response, and then translate it back into one of my native tongues. It was a lengthy and confusing process, and no matter how much I begged, the doctors wouldn't let me leave the hospital standing…not even on crutches.

"We don't want you to fall." was all they'd ever say. "When your balance is better, you don't have to use the wheelchair. But until then, Carline…use the wheelchair!"

When we left, my parents and I had a plan. I had a list of exercises I was not allowed to do, a list of ones that would be safe for me, a sample diet, and the wheelchair I hated so much. All of these things, I was told, would help me on my journey to regain my strength. I was more than ready to go home. I was ready to take the next step toward the destiny God had planned for my life.

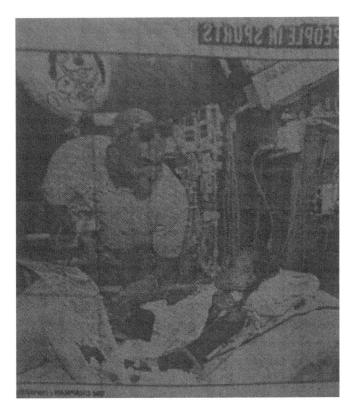

Carline gets a surprise visit from the *Miami Heat* while recovering from her first heart surgery

CHAPTER 6

*Living in the Aftermath*

It was strange for me…going home after I had been in the hospital for so long. I was full of hope that my life would get back to normal, but in the midst of that, I couldn't help but wonder what "normal" would even look like. My home now was not the one that was filled with so many colorful memories of homemade tonics from my mother's expensive lotions, or the beautiful Haitian weather that I loved so much. I wouldn't be surrounded by the warm and friendly people I'd known all my life; instead, I was surrounded by foreign Americans whom I had nothing in common with. I couldn't even eat my favorite foods now that I was on the new Cardiac diet. Nothing was the same. There I was, in a new, foreign country without the familiarity of friends and daily life to cling to, and I was expected to learn how to function again.

More than anything, I wanted to step away from the life of survival that I'd always known. I wanted to live. I wanted to thrive.

I wanted to be a normal girl again. I wanted to go to school, make new friends, and explore, and run, and jump. I was ready to do anything and everything that I took for granted before I got sick. The desire to take back what I had lost drove me to move around as much as I could— independently— and to do my little physical therapy exercises on a daily basis. I would consciously practice the subconscious movements most people don't have to think about: things like breathing exercises, hand strengthening techniques, and leg stretches. I was mindful of each and every movement and did them in perpetuity. In my mind, if I could build up my strength and heal my body, I could get back to the way things were before I got sick. I knew I had to pick a goal to strive for, something that I wanted bad enough to push myself for.

My goal was to go back to school.

During my sickness and recovery, my parents made the decision to homeschool me. Looking back, I know it made sense to continue my education while I couldn't physically attend school, but during that time…Ohhhh…*I hated it*. My normally effervescent personality was stifled by the lack of interaction with peers. I missed the hustle of girlfriend gossip by the bathroom, recess, and the camaraderie that comes from sitting in a class together, all struggling to understand a new concept. My parents did their best to make my homeschooling environment as enjoyable as possible for me, but it was no substitution for the joy I had always taken in going to school. My siblings weren't homeschooled with me, and it was difficult for me to watch them go to school, something that seemingly no other child in America wanted to do…everyday felt like I was missing out on the best thing in the world.

I watched enviously as my siblings continued about their lives with no interruption from heart trouble. I constantly asked, 'Why me? Why me and not my siblings? Why is this my cross to bear?' I wondered if perhaps, in time, I would grow to understand God's purpose in my life for all the sickness and pain I had to endure. But at the time, I just needed to do whatever I could to grow and fight the state of health I was in. I told myself that I would one day be normal. I would.

Physical Therapy lasted around six months after my surgery, and I had to use the wheelchair for close to a year. When I had been out of the hospital for six weeks, I went for my first Cardiologist post-op visit. I was back in the hospital, sitting down in another bare white wall, and stuck in the same building I'd tried so desperately to escape. The Cardiologist walked into the room and smiled at me. He checked my chart and looked at the medications I was on, and inspected the surgical site.

"So," he asked, as he went about the routine. "How is everything going?"

I knew I had no room to complain. I was healthy, healing, and alive. I knew that I shouldn't be unhappy, but I was. I missed interacting and playing with kids my own age. Before I could stop it, the truth I had been wrestling with for so long spilled out of me.

"It's hard. I miss school. I'm tired of being sick. I don't like having to do all this. I wish I was a normal kid."

I saw his head nod, and for a brief moment, panic flashed through me. Suddenly scared, I quickly explained that I had been doing my daily exercises.

"I'm doing all the steps and I'm eating the right foods."

"Uh, huh."

"It's just a lot. I miss having a social life. And I really want to go back to school."

He chuckled. It must have seemed funny to him, that the thing I wanted the most was to go back to school, and I wanted it desperately.

I am forever grateful that he was kind and thoughtful about my request. He explained to me the potential dangers of rushing through my recovery. He told me how easily I could get hurt. He could have dismissed me right then and there, but instead, he took a long look at my plaintive little face.

"Well, then…Carline…do you think you'll recover if you continue to do all the right steps?"

I had my eyes glued on the doctor but my ears only heard the translator.

"I think it'll work…I know it'll work."

"You think you'll recover?" he asked.

"Yes."

"Without a doubt?"

I nodded my head emphatically.

"Yes."

I waited anxiously for the translator to finish his last words.

"I'll tell you what," the doctor said, leaning forward on his swivel chair. "I'll make a deal with you. If you are good about doing your home therapy on a daily basis…and your strength and mobility shows significant improvement, then I will allow you to return to school."

I was overjoyed. The keys to freedom were nearly in my reach. My goal felt closer than ever, and I was grateful to the doctor for his consideration. Every day for the next three months, I pushed myself to do everything. I walked up and down the hallway of my new home and I pushed myself to do it for longer sessions every day. Slowly but surely, my strength returned, and I was finally able to go back to school.

My first day back was a blitz of nerves and excitement. I had the same nervous energy that any child has on their first day at a new school. That feeling of excitement— bubbling on the edge of fear…the one that makes you feel like you might vomit— was not unfamiliar to me. I was used to that nervous, queasy feeling in the pit of my stomach, but this time it was different than before.

*So what is it that is so different this time? What is this new feeling of anxiety I'm struggling with? Will my disease set me apart from my classmates? What if they ostracize me? Will they see my health issues hovering over me like a veil? If they do, will they treat me differently?*

These concerns never stopped, and they followed me throughout the remainder of middle school and all of high school. My bubbly and friendly disposition changed when I was in school. I went from a friendly social butterfly to a rather quiet, timid, and introverted person. I felt like my classmates and I were distanced from each other. As much as I wanted to belong, my condition often robbed me of experiencing school the way my peers did. It was easy for them to make spontaneous plans, go on sleepovers, and throw everything they had into sports and activities. I, on the other hand, would always have to be mindful of my heart and balance my school work with my lifelong doctor visits. It's hard to fit in when all your friends are worrying about making the cheer team while you're worrying about whether or not your heart check up at the end of the month will say you're good enough to stay in school.

Instead of allowing the distance I felt between me and my classmates to weigh me down, I often poured my heart out in writing. I scribbled away in a notebook filled with poetry and diary entries. As a more private person, I was never as interested in social gatherings, so reading, writing, and spending time at home was just as enjoyable to me as going to school soccer games and Friday night football. With my condition stable enough that my life was close to normal, my creativity returned, and it gave me an outlet for any overwhelming sadness derived from feeling like I wasn't 'one of the girls.'

While I was at home, I would watch my mother work. She was a seamstress once again, and watching her work became a ritualistic experience for me. I loved the way she could take a yard of flat fabric and turn it into a beautiful outfit. With steady hands, she would create and refurbish dresses, and I would watch her, wide-eyed and fascinated. Watching her work so hard gave me a deep desire to focus on my own education. It gave me both an eye and a love for fashion. Growing up, I would design fancy dresses for my dolls. I'd create makeshift runways, and make my dolls catwalk and model my designs. It always gave me such a rush of joy. There was something healing in the simple fact that even I could create something beautiful. As I grew older and put away my dolls, I still held tight to that feeling. I recognized that in the same way I loved creating something from nothing with my dolls, God also loved creating something with my life that I would never have expected to happen.

I tried to keep this in mind throughout my adolescence. God had a plan for me that was beyond my understanding. Part of me wanted to translate 'God's plan' to mean that the Lord would only allow good things to happen in my life from here on out. I wanted to believe that with every fiber of my being. I was tired of the bad news, health scares, and the continuing comments from my doctors on how much my disease was truly taking from me. It was draining, and I wasn't sure how much more of my heart condition I could take.

# CHAPTER 7

## *Curfews*

Once I was eighteen and legally an adult, I started going to my checkups alone. My parents stopped making sure I was taking my medication at the same time every day, twice a day. I was still a kid in many ways, and I often forgot to take my morning doses. When I finally did remember several hours later, I'd run and take my meds. When nighttime came, I'd waited so long to take the first round of medication that it was too close to take my second round of the nighttime medication. On my best days, I took one pill midday.

Even though I still wasn't allowed to spend the night or date, and my nightly curfew was at eight o'clock, I was allowed to leave and hang out with my friends. After high school, I started attending cosmetology school and I often spent time at friend's houses doing hair and makeup. My friends would line up, and I'd spend all my time braiding and styling their hair into intricate designs. We'd talk and chat, and I loved every second of it. There were times I'd get so caught up in the conversation, that I almost missed curfew. I'd rush back home and slip in just before my dad locked the gate.

I love my father, but he ran our house like a well oiled machine. I'd lived so much of my life without him, that it was almost strange to adhere to his rules. I did, of course, because I loved my parents and didn't want to cause strife, but the rules were restrictive, and it made me feel even more ostracized than I already was from the other girls my age. Strict curfew, no dating, and a very modest dress code that kept me in long jean skirts until I left my parent's house.

But the curfew was the cause of many terrifying (now amusing) and stressful experiences. Us kids weren't the only ones who suffered because of the dreaded curfew. My mother got locked out of the house on more than one occasion. No one came into the house without going through my father. We had a gate that went all the way around our house, so if the gate was locked, there was no way in. My older brother was agile enough to jump over the fence, and I was often woken by the noise of my brother tapping on my window.

"Carline! Let me in! I'm locked out!"

Then I'd open the window, my brother would crawl through, and he'd sneak back off to his room. My parents had no idea, and this is probably the first time they'll hear of it. Even though my brother could get away with it, I couldn't. I would have liked to, but with my heart, my condition was fragile. It took me a long time after the surgery to be able to walk normally, but eventually I did. Even though I had healed from the surgery, I wasn't physically strong enough to jump over the gate. And even if there was a tiny chance that I had enough strength and could jump over the gate on both my way out and on my way back in, I didn't want to risk it. I saw no reason why I should risk my relatively stable health for another stay at the hospital.

But I still got locked out.

Our church was having a revival night, and my mother and I sat in church. We had about two hours or so before we had to leave to make curfew, so we decided to stick around a little while longer and stay through the end of the sermon. After all, it would only take us fifteen minutes to get home, so we had plenty of time. No reason to panic. But as the sermon went on, and the pastor got more and more into the sermon, I nervously started glancing at the clock. The pastor's preaching was so intense, and it was all I could do to keep up with his rapid teaching, but after years of the eight o'clock curfew, it was second nature to keep one eye on the clock at all times.

"Mom," I said. "Mom, it's going long. We should probably leave soon."

My mother ignored me. *Completely* ignored me. The woman didn't even turn her head toward me.

"Mom, we really gotta go."

Still, she said nothing. I was starting to get nervous, but it wasn't like I could have left without her. Knowing we were going to be late and we were going to get locked out anyway, I sat back in the pew, and listened to the rest of the sermon.

Sure enough, we were late, and the gate was locked long before we walked up. From outside the gate, I could see my father, calmly sitting in the living room. He turned his head, and looked at me. He just stared. I waved to him, then jiggled the gate door.

Nothing.

My father was petty enough to sit there, in the living room, and just stare at us. He knew we were there. *We* knew, that *he* knew, that *we were there*, and we *all* knew that *he* wasn't going to let us in.

We stood outside for at least twenty minutes before my father finally came to the front door. He opened the door, walked outside very slowly, and made his way over to us. He looked at us, and pretended to be confused.

"Have fun at church?"

"Yes, we did." my mother said. "Let us in."

"Huh." my father responded, and pretended to think. "You just got here?"

"No!" my mother said, her voice rising a little. "We've been standing here for the past twenty minutes. Let us in!"

"No, no." my father shook his head. "You just got here a minute ago."

"No, we did not!" my mother yelled. "Open up this gate!"

And eventually, he did let us inside. I walked back to my room, and I could still hear my parents yelling in the kitchen.

"Why did the pastor take so long?" my father asked.

My mother threw her hands up.

"How should I know? Should I have asked him? Should I have thrown up my hands in the middle of service and said, 'Pastor, why are you taking so long? Can you hurry up please, because my husband needs me at home.' You wanted me to do that in the middle of revival night?"

"Yes!" my father nodded, his voice just as loud as my mother's. "Yes, you should have told him!"

"Okay, next time I will just leave in the middle of service. I'll just get up and leave. I'll stand up, in the middle of revival night, and just walk out. Right during service. Is that what you want?"

"Yes!" my father shouted.

"Fine! I will!"

"Fine!"

"Fine!"

Then, right in the middle of fighting, my parents would stop arguing, and in a split second, they'd immediately switch off their attitudes and be very playful with each other. My father would ask my mother to scratch his back, and she would do so.

"No, no. Not there. Lower. Lower."

"Where? Right here?" my mother would ask, scratching where he indicated.

"Ah, yes, perfect. Right there."

Then my mother would stop scratching his back, and sometimes they'd go back to fighting, and sometimes they'd move on like the argument never happened in the first place. That's my parents for you. They could be petty and strict and strike the fear of God in you, and then laugh it off and move on. That's my family, and I love them.

*Carline at her high school graduation*

# CHAPTER 8

## *My First and Last Time in the Club*

And as for the times where *I* actually *did* get locked out?

It was right after I got out of high school. One of my closest friends, Vicky, invited me out for a house party. I thought it'd be fun, and I'd see all my friends and braid a few girl's hair. I didn't dare ask my father for permission, and instead, I went directly to my mother. She still made us follow the rules, but she was much more relaxed in her approach.

"Now, Carline," she would say, acting very serious. "You know the rules. You know that you have to be back before curfew, or you're going to get locked out…and you know I'm not going to help you. I'm not going to get in between you and your father like that. If you get locked out, you're on your own. Don't come crying to me. So go and have fun, just come back before curfew, ya hear?"

I'd nod and thank her, and I'd run out before my father could stop me and say otherwise. In this particular instance, Vicky came over to my house, picked me up, and took me to the house party. We were there way too early, but Vicky assured me that there would be more people soon. But for the next hour and a half, it was just me, Vicky, and some other women in the kitchen who were still cooking and setting up for the party.

"Vicky, if I wanted to do nothing I would have sat at home. This is dumb. Nobody is here."

"Okay, Carline, okay." she said, trying to calm me down. "Don't worry, Kah, Baby Daddy is looking for another house party for us to go to."

Vicky had been dating her boyfriend for several years, and although she didn't have any kids with him (or any kids at all, for that matter), she found it very amusing to call him Baby Daddy. So that's what we all called him, Baby Daddy.

Baby Daddy showed up and said he'd take us to another house party. He told me it'd be fun, that he was friends with the host, and that I'd still have enough time to make it back before my curfew, but I was still hesitant.

"Baby Daddy, I don't know any of your friends, and I have to be home in time for curfew."

"Ayyy, Kah," Vicky told me, trying to convince me that I was overreacting. "It'll be fun. Don't worry."

"Vicky," I said. "Vicky, listen. I don't know his friends. I don't feel comfortable going. You know my parents. I don't want to get in trouble."

Baby Daddy turned around and looked at me sitting in the back of the car. He shook his head.

"It won't be long, Kah, okay? We'll go, we'll hang out just for a bit, and then we'll leave. Okay? I'll take you back home. Your parents don't need to know."

Begrudgingly, I agreed, and Baby Daddy drove us to the house party. As soon as we got there, I knew something wasn't right. First off, it wasn't a residential neighborhood, and I wondered if maybe the house party was catty-corner to one of the businesses. I'd never been to the friend's house before, so I didn't know. I thought perhaps maybe we were taking a shortcut, or coming into the house through the back way.

But that's not what happened.

Baby Daddy led me and Vicky to a building with a long line and a crowd of people hanging out by the entrance.

We took a step inside, and the air was completely covered in hazy fog. It was loud. It was so loud that I couldn't hear what Vicky was saying, and she was right next to me. She was yelling, and I still couldn't hear anything. The reggae music blasted through the speakers and it was only a matter of seconds before my ears ached.

I already felt uneasy, and before I could object to Vicky further, my eyes flashed, and I saw people ducking down. Shots were going off all throughout the club, and people were spread out all over the club floor, clinging to the ground. I saw people getting hurt and killed.

As quickly as it had happened, it was over. I knew instantly that I'd just had a vision, and I had a bad feeling. It was making me sick to my stomach, and I tugged on Vicky's arm. I knew I couldn't tell her that I had a vision, because she'd think I was crazy, so I begged her to go and told her the reason was that I was afraid I'd get terrible asthma and wouldn't be able to breathe.

"This isn't a house party!" I yelled.

"What?!?" Vicky yelled back.

"Vicky, we have to go. There's too much smoke here."

And it was true. There *was* too much smoke in the club, and it was only a matter of time before it made me sick. I didn't want to go back into the hospital. It didn't take very much to get me into a hospital bed, but it took what felt like forever to get me out of one.

"Kah, relax. It's going to be fine." Vicky told me, playing it off. "We'll stay, we'll talk to some people, and we'll have you home before curfew."

"But, Vicky!" I yelled into her ear, and it still sounded like a whisper by comparison. "I don't feel comfortable here. I think we should go. It's not safe here."

Baby Daddy put his arm around Vicky's shoulder, and they both looked at me like I was crazy. He shrugged, and looked around the club.

"Twenty minutes, okay? Twenty minutes and we can go. Just have a good time." he said.

And that was that. I was stuck there. They were my ride, so I couldn't leave on my own. I tried to breathe as little as I could. I'd wait the twenty minutes and Vicky and Baby Daddy would take me home.

We didn't even make it to twenty minutes.

We'd barely been in the club for ten minutes. Baby Daddy was introducing me to one of his friends who also happened to be at the club. They'd been talking for a few minutes, and I stood nearby and listened while my eyes wandered around the club. I looked over to the bar, and saw a large, tall Jamaican man with dreads yell at the bartender. The bartender yelled something back, and Jamaican man grabbed a heavy bottle of wine, and knocked him on the head!

The man fell down, and then a loud BANG! The noise cut through the club, filling it with the screams of the club patrons against the ever blaring reggae music in the background. Just like in my vision, everyone panicked, and dropped to the floor. Baby Daddy's friend got our attention, and told us he knew a way out. We crawled on our stomachs and followed him. He showed us a small, back entrance out of the club. We ran through it, and didn't stop running until we reached the car. As soon as we got into the car and started the engine, police sirens sounded behind us, and whooshed by to the club, followed by a news team. If we'd been just a few seconds slower, I would have ended up all over the news. Me, the church girl in the long jean skirt would have been reported on the news as an eyewitness to a club shooting. My parents would have put the fear of God in me the moment they found out.

They took me home. I had a few minutes before curfew, but I didn't want to risk it. I ran into the house, and the first thing I did was grab a plastic bag. My clothes were overpowered with smoke, and the last thing I needed was to get caught with smoke on my clothes. I'd never hear the end of it. I stripped down, and put my clothes in the plastic bag. I double knotted it, and immediately ran and took a shower, scrubbing down with handfuls of soap until I couldn't smell it anymore. I changed into my pajamas, grabbed the bag, and threw it in the trash cans outside. I came back into the house and slipped into bed. I was breathing heavy, and was so afraid I'd get caught. It was a little hard for me to breathe, but I still managed to get to sleep.

I didn't sleep very well, and in the morning, I knew I needed to go to the hospital. I left by myself and was admitted immediately. I told the doctor it was hard for me to breathe, and because they knew who I was and all the health problems I had, that admitted me without question. They ran some tests and took a chest x-ray of my lungs. I waited in my room until the doctor walked back in, holding the results of my x-rays.

"Hello." he said.

"Hi."

He kicked his swivel stool over and sat down next to my bed. He flipped open the folder, and took out the x-rays. He held them up for me to see. I knew I was about to get lectured big time. I had a suspicious of what the x-rays had found.

"Carline," he said. "Why are you smoking?"

"Smoking? Me? Smoking? I don't smoke."

"Carline, we can see that there's smoke all over your lungs. You know better than that." he said, and shook his head. "You can't smoke! Your heart condition is very serious! You must stop smoking!"

I tried to think of something to say. Anything to say that wouldn't be a lie, but also wouldn't get back to my parents.

"Oh, no, no. That's not it. You, see, what had happened was…" I chose my words very carefully, knowing that it would find its way back to my parents eventually. "I was *around* people who smoked. That must have been what happened…yes. Yes, that was it. I went to a, uh, a house party, and I was just *around* people that smoked. That's all."

"You were *around* people who smoked?"

"Yes," I said, nodding fervently. "It wasn't me. It was…everyone else."

"Carline!" he said sternly, furrowing his brow. "You know better than to be around smoke! Don't you know that secondhand smoke is even worse for you than the person who is smoking it?"

"…I did not."

"Carline…Carline you really have to be more careful."

"Absolutely." I nodded. "I will absolutely be more careful from now on. I will never be around smoke again."

I'm still not sure if he believed me or not, but that was the last of the smoke talk. We went on to talk about my medications. I didn't even have to admit to being bad about taking them, because the doctor could tell simply by looking at my blood work. Because I hadn't been good about taking my blood thinners, my blood was far more clotted than it should have been. I was going to have to stay in the hospital for about a week until both the problems with my blood and lungs had been worked out.

My parents came to see me later that day, and while they were on their way up, I was certain that the doctor had told them what happened, and then I'd be forced to tell them the truth about last night. Much to my surprise, he said nothing, and my family (until now) had no idea why exactly I'd gone to the hospital in the first place.

And that was my first and last time in a club.

Vicky and I had many adventures together, though they weren't all that exciting. She did, however, get me a job at *Burger King*, which nearly ended the same way.

Vicky would always talk about how much money she made and how much she loved having a job…even if it was just cashiering. Though we were still in high school at the time, it seemed everyone around me was getting a job and moving on with their lives.

"You want a job, Kah? I got you. I know the manager over at Burger King. I'll tell him to give you a job."

"You know I really want one," I said. "But how can I get a job with my condition?"

She waved me off, laughing.

"Girl, it's a cashier job. You just stand at the register and take people's money and then hand them their food. You can do that, can't you?"

"Well," I started, racking my brain to see if any other problems might be associated with cashiering. "yes…yes, I can do that."

She clapped her hands excitedly and smiled.

"Girl, you hired!"

My first shift started the next week. It wasn't too long, just a few hours or so, but it was more than enough for me. My dad dropped me off in the afternoon, and I told him I'd be off around eight. He wasn't thrilled that I'd gotten a job, but he was going to let me try it, and I didn't want to do anything that might make him change his mind.

The shift passed uneventfully, and the manager locked up the lobby. I handed my drawer back to the shift manager and tidied up my station. Through the lobby windows, I saw the headlights of my dad's car. I said goodbye to the crew and walked toward the exit doors.

"Where do you think you're going?"

I turned around to see the manager— a middle aged man— frowning down at me. He tapped his foot impatiently and crossed his arms.

"Home. My shift is over. So…I'm going home."

He looked at me like I was stupid. Then he sighed, unfolded his arms, and shook his head.

"You can't leave until you clean the lobby."

"Clean the lobby?"

*Clean? I don't even clean my own house! Mom does all the cleaning!*

Needless to say, I was very spoiled.

"Yes, you have to mop." he retorted.

"Mop?" I asked, panic setting in. "I have to mop? But I'm a cashier!"

"So?" he asked, impatiently. "It's in your job description."

"Sir," I said. "I can't mop. I wasn't told anything about mopping. I can't mop. I have a hear—"

He walked over to the corner of the lobby where the mop was balancing against the ledge of a table, grabbed it, and brought it back over to me. He looked at me, then at the mop, then back at me.

"Go on." he said. "Mop."

"But—" I started.

"Mop, and then you can go home." he told me, before he walked away.

I looked at the mop, then to my father's car, and then back to the mop. I contemplated what I should do, only to end up grabbing the mop and attempting to mop without seriously injuring myself. Because of my heart condition, there were certain movements that I couldn't do, and while it seems strange and unrelated, mopping (or sweeping, for that matter) used too many shoulder and chest muscles when pushing and pulling the mop back and forth across the floor— it was something I avoided at all costs.

But I really wanted that paycheck.

It didn't take long before my father rushed up to the door and started pounding on the window. This brought the manager back out to the lobby, where he promptly yelled at him through the double glass doors.

"Sir! Sir! We're not open! We're closed!"

"I know that!" my father shouted back.

"Then go home!" the manager yelled.

My father completely ignored him, and continued pounding on the glass. The manager grew more and more worried, and I realized I should probably say something before he called the cops.

"Uh, actually, that's my dad. He's here to pick me up."

"Oh," the manager said, still looking puzzled. "Um, okay then."

He crossed the lobby and unlocked the doors, let my father inside, and immediately apologized.

"Sorry, sir. I didn't know you were Carline's dad. I thought you were a customer."

The manager got no response, and my father instead looked at me, squinting his eyes. I already knew what he was going to say.

"Girl, what are you doing?"

"I'm…mopping. Cashiers have to mop…apparently it's part of the job description. I didn't know that."

My father shook his head. He pointed to the manager.

"She can't be doing that. She's got a condition."

The manager shrugged.

"She has to mop. All the cashiers mop. They're responsible for cleaning the lobby so that our morning shift can—"

"No, no." my father continued. "You don't understand. She can't be mopping. It'll make her sick."

"Sir, she has to mop. I'm in charge here and I have to enforce the rules and keep the staff in line. And I say she has to sweep because that's the rules."

"Carline," my father said. "Carline, get your stuff. Let's go."

"Sir!" the manager exclaimed. "Sir, she has to mop the floor before she can—"

"No." my father said. "I said she's not mopping. Let's go."

The manager looked like he was at a loss for words, but it didn't last long.

"Listen, you might be Carline's dad, but I am Carline's boss, and in order for her to keep this job, she has to mop this floor…tonight and every other night or I'll be forced to fire her."

"Fine." my father shrugged. "Carline, you're fired. Let's go."

"But…but *I'm* the manager. *You* can't fire her…*I* have to fire her…you don't have the authority to do that and she has to—"

"And I'm her father, and I say she's fired, so she's fired and that's that. Now we're going to leave."

"But what about my check?" I asked. "How am I going to get my check if we leave before I can—"

"Leave it! Who cares. Just leave it and forget about it. I knew this was a bad idea. You should be in school. You should be focusing on your assignments and your homework, not mopping some fast food floor. Is this what you want to do with the rest of your life? Mopping someone else's floor? No! I won't allow it! Get in the car."

And then we walked out of the lobby, got into the car, and never came back.

I had a few other odd jobs, but no more in the fast food industry, thankfully. Another job that was equally as terrible as *Burger King*, was my short lived employment at a debt collection call center.

I was given my headset and the company script and sat down in the corner with a call list. I was supposed to call, introduce myself, make sure I had the correct person on the phone before I divulged any account information, and tell them the reason I was calling. We were told that we had to follow the script as closely as possible. It was an easy script to follow, so it didn't seem all that difficult. They asked if I had anymore questions, I told them I didn't, and then I dialed the first number on the list.

It only rang twice before a thick, gruff accent answered the phone.

"Hello?"

"Hi, yes, my name is Carline and I'm with the Banks and Simons Collection Agency. Is Siddharth Ansh Davuluri Jr. there?"

"Yeah, sure. What do you want from me?"

"Like I said sir, I'm with the Banks and Simons Collection Agency and I see that your account is currently $428.96 past due and I was just looking to collect on that."

Then the conversation turned hostile, and there was nothing in the script about how to handle *yourself* when dealing with an irate debtor.

"Okay, how can I help you?" he shouted through the phone.

"I'm just trying to collect on that debt—"

"You know what you are?!" he screamed. "You're just a thief! You're just a thief! That's all you are! A thief! I work hard for my money and I won't let anyone take it away from me! Do you understand?!"

He howled through the phone. You'd think that because I grew up in a similar aggressive culture (both Haitians and Indians have a tendency to be incredibly harsh) that I would have been well equipped to deal with this kind of situation.

But I wasn't.

I cried like a baby. Needless to say, I didn't work as a collector much longer after that.

# CHAPTER 9

## *Crushed Dreams*

I hit my breaking point when I was visiting my doctor and he finally told me that, due to my condition, I could not have children. He went on to tell me that even if I did somehow conceive, it would be a high-risk pregnancy that could lead to death for both myself and the baby. Best case scenario, any child I had would be born with Down syndrome. There was no 'maybe' from the doctor that day; I was never going to have children. I was devastated. I was completely blindsided because I did not go into my appointment expecting to hear this kind of news. It was supposed to be just another checkup. I didn't go to the doctor expecting anything like that. What I thought would be a routine visit ended up crushing one of my dreams.

Like most girls, I have always wanted to meet my Prince Charming, fall in love, get married, and have beautiful babies. As I sat in the office, trying to digest that I might never have the future I dreamed of, my doctor delivered more bad news.

"Your mitral valve was only a temporary replacement."

I blinked, still trying to process the fact that I'd never have children.

The doctor continued.

"We needed to know the approximate duration. This was always the plan. Based on how well you took care of yourself, if you took your medications on time, and if you were good about keeping up with your follow-up appointments…things like that. These are the things that would give us a clue for how long this particular valve would last."

"I need another valve?"

"Yes. You'll still need to have more surgeries in the future as well. Think of it as upkeep."

While the doctor tried to soften the blow by reminding me that until I needed my surgeries, I could always travel and continue enjoying life, it didn't take away the sting of his words. I could never have a normal life. All the things I had ever hoped and dreamed for as a little girl were now dead. I cried myself to sleep that night, and for many nights that followed.

I grieved for the life I wanted to live, and then, in the darkness, I lost sight of why life is worth living. I had fought so hard, over and over again, only to be defeated once more. I would never be free of my illness, and I didn't want to live as a prisoner anymore.

*I can't go on like this. What other bad news is just around the corner? What is the point of living if none of my dreams come true?*

One night, while the rest of my family was asleep, I decided to make a desperate attempt to free myself. I grabbed ten or fifteen of my blood thinner pills and chased them down with a glass of water.

As my heart started racing and my chest felt heavy, I remember thinking that I was going to die. This was it. This was going to help me escape it all. Why else would I have taken so many pills?

*This is what I wanted, isn't it?*

But as it became more and more difficult to breathe, I realized I didn't want to die. I wasn't ready. I had so much to live for! There were so many reasons to keep going. There were people who needed me. What would my parents do when they found my body in the morning? How would my siblings feel when I wasn't there for them anymore?

Panic gripped me as my mind raced.

*It was too late.*

That night, I vividly saw the death I had so willingly created for myself. Slow, isolated, and painful. I closed my eyes, sure that I would never open them again. In my fear, I cried out to God. I begged him to forgive me. I pleaded with Him to give me another chance not only to live, but to live right by Him. With each struggled intake of breath, I realized that suicide is never the answer. Life is difficult and painful, but it is always worth living. As the darkness I thought would be eternal enveloped me, I repented of my sin.

In the morning, I woke up drowsy, weak, and shocked. God had intervened on my behalf again. He had saved me for the third time. My parents did not know why I stayed in bed that day, and I never mentioned anything to anyone. It was a miracle that I kept to myself. God had spared me, and I wasn't going to take it lightly. From that day on, I embraced the life I was given and committed to walking on my wellness path without too much complaining.

Now, I can honestly say that I am honored to be living life and I thank God for the second chances He provides to us over and over again. I gave myself permission to be good enough and not perfect, because no one is, and no one ever will be perfect. Though people may smile and appear happy on the outside, they have been through every bit as much chaos in their own lives, but they choose to use the courage and strength God gave them to smile through it anyway. I learned that your past is important to learn from as well as your future is important to work toward. But I learned that I must choose to live in the present, and that is what I have done since that day.

# CHAPTER 10

*First Love*

I didn't get out much, and when I did, it was to church. I had a friend who was Seventh Day Adventist, and she'd frequently invite me to her church's events. I went every so often and hung out with her and the other girls and the church's youth group. I was a 'member' in everything but name.

The church my family attended was a Baptist church, and it was far less fun. My home church didn't have fun youth groups, and they never took us anywhere outside of church. But the Adventist church…they'd take us to places like *Six Flags* and *Disney World*. These were the kind of places I never dreamed I'd be able to go to, definitely not with my parents and certainly not with the church. So when the Adventists told me that I could no longer continue to participate in their events and services unless I was baptized into their church, I barely hesitated.

I'd been baptized before, of course, but I didn't mention it to them. After they baptized me, they gave me a little baptism certificate. I placed it in the cover of my Bible, set my Bible on my nightstand, and didn't think much more about it. But my mother— as mothers always do— eventually found it. She was cleaning my room and was moving things around so she could vacuum. Somehow, the certificate fell out of my Bible and she picked it up.

"Carline!"

"Yes, mom?" I called back, from the other end of the house.

"Come here."

"Why? What's wrong?"

"Carline, just get in your room."

I left what I was doing, stood up, and walked down the hall to my room, where I was greeted by my frowning mother.

"What's this?" she demanded, and shoved the certificate in my hand.

"Ohhhh…Oh, *that*." I said, stalling for time. "That's, uh, um, a baptism certificate."

"I can see *that*, Carline. I have eyes."

"Okay…?"

I stared up at her, waiting for the inevitable rain of fire.

"Did you tell them you were baptized before? Did you tell them that, Carline? Hmmmm?"

"Uh…no. It didn't come up, no."

She smirked.

"Then they didn't really baptize you, now did they?"

"No, no…" I said. "They did, they gave me the certificate." I explained, waving it in front of her face as if she'd forgotten what started this whole mess. "See?"

"But it doesn't count."

"It doesn't count?" I parroted.

She shook her head.

"You were already baptized, so the second time doesn't count. They just gave you a bath."

"Huh?"

"It doesn't count. They just dipped you in water and gave you a bath. You can't get baptized twice. You might as well have taken a bath. It doesn't count."

"Okay, but…" I started to think up an excuse, but she cut me off before I could get it out.

"It was a bath, Carline." she insisted, then waved me off. "Now go away. I'm cleaning."

I may have spent most of my time at church, but like every young woman, the thing I looked forward to the most in life was falling in love. I longed for the day my Prince Charming would sweep me off my feet, and we would ride away into the sunset together. I wanted the kind of romance and unshakable connection that I saw in movies. It took me far too long to realize that I already had the kind of unconditional love I craved. If I had only sat still in the presence of God, I would have realized that He was everything I needed, more than I could ever hope for, and everything I longed for. With the Lord, I didn't need to hope for a relationship to fill the longing in my heart; I already had everything I needed. Unfortunately, like many young women, I didn't realize that until it was too late.

Instead of being content, I eagerly waited for Mr. Right. I thought finding him would solve all of my problems. The first time I met someone who I thought could be "the one," I fell hard and fast for his charismatic personality. The day we met, I was singing at a youth conference. I'll never forget the way he swaggered up to me and my friend, a broad smile lit up his face. My best friend and I were getting some snacks and drinks, enjoying a brief intermission from the conference. I wasn't there to meet any boys. In fact, I wasn't even allowed to date at the time. My parents had firm rules about dating and relationships, as well as strict guidelines for the types of activities I could do. Dating was not one of them.

Now, as an adult, I'm grateful for their guidance. It would have been all too easy for me to get swept away by the flash of materialism or the allure of sin as a teenager. Every young person is a target for being led astray. As a parent, I understand that now, but as a teenager, I wished they were less restricting. So, when a family friend agreed to watch out for me at the youth conference where he and his band were also performing, I knew the best thing I could do for myself was to stay out of trouble. But when that young man sauntered up to me and my friend at the refreshment stand, I knew without a doubt he was trouble.

He was so confident, it made me sure that he had to be smiling at someone else. I wasn't looking for a relationship— or even a friendship— with a strange boy, so why would he be interested in me?

It was only when he said, "Hello beautiful ladies, may I join you guys?" that I realized his smile might have been for me.

I remember thinking that he was either one of the bravest or one of the most brazen men I had ever met, jumping into a stranger's conversation like that. Little bells went off in my mind. I knew my father wouldn't approve. He didn't approve of me talking with any boys besides my brothers, and I definitely wasn't allowed to have a boyfriend until I graduated college. But the way he looked at me, like I was a prize just waiting to be won, or a stallion ready to be broken in, was unlike anything I had ever experienced before. It made my heart race. Looking back, I wish I could have stepped out of my body and looked at the experience differently. I would have seen the red flags. When your family tries to protect you from something, it's often better to heed their wise counsel even if you do not understand their reasoning at that exact moment.

When he asked me for my number so we could talk on the phone, I struggled to understand why my father didn't want me to start dating. A part of me wanted to give him my number. I wanted to taste what it was like to walk on the wild side. This stranger didn't look at me like I was fragile. There was no pity for the girl with the heart defect, only curiosity and something akin to longing. Heart thundering in my chest, I explained to him that even if I did give him my number— which I wanted to, but didn't admit— we wouldn't be able to talk on the phone. My father only allowed me to speak to my best friend and my immediate family.

I expected him to scoff at me, possibly tease me for my father's overprotectiveness, but instead, he just smiled like he enjoyed the challenge. He scribbled down his number so I could call him. I wasn't sure if I would call him or not. I wasn't sure if I would refuse his advances, or just tuck his number away as a reminder that not everyone in the world saw me as a sick little girl. Unfortunately, I never got a chance to see what happened. My chaperone/family friend walked up, snatched his number, and firmly scolded both myself and the young man. After he had dismissed him, he turned to me and threatened to tell my father what happened.

For the rest of the conference, and several weeks after it, I waited to see what would happen when my father found out. Luckily for me, our family friend decided against telling my father. I didn't think about the stranger at the conference often. I allowed myself to focus on anything but falling in love. I assumed that whenever I did fall in love, it would be fate. However, two years later, when I once again ran into the young man when I went to visit a church, it wasn't the fate that I thought had pulled us together. He must have, though, because the first thing he said to me was, "Small world," and then he smiled his signature grin. Once again, he didn't hesitate to give me his number.

This time there was no chaperone to intervene, but his allure seemed tainted to me. I knew he was still trouble and I wasn't interested. I never called him. It was only when I ran into him again, three years after our second meeting and five years after the conference, that I wondered if maybe fate *was* trying to tell me something. This time, when he asked for my number, I gave it to him. We talked for six months before we started dating. We dated for three good years and almost got married. Our relationship blossomed, but I was saving myself for marriage, and so was he. We truly wanted to honor God with our bodies. He was my first love, but our short lived engagement didn't last long. The relationship was pressured continuously by family issues and his own insecurities. When we finally broke up, I thought I had lost the only person I could ever love.

# CHAPTER 11

## *Prince Charming*

My heart was broken, and I was left wondering how I would heal. Five months later, I thought I met the person who God sent to help heal my heart. Little did I know, not everyone who enters our lives can heal us, no matter how much we want them to. There are those who can help us grow. They will sharpen us as iron sharpens iron; through love and encouragement, they will build us up and never tear us down. There are, however, those who are so damaged that they can not help others, they can only hurt them.

Learning to see the difference between those two types of people is extremely difficult. It takes wisdom and discernment from the Lord, and is part of something we all must learn on our own at our own pace. I wish that I would have waited quietly for the Lord to answer my questions about my now ex-husband, instead of getting swept away when I met him. But I let my heart guide me instead of the Lord. I acted on emotions that can so easily change. Like the seasons, love and strong emotions can change without warning, and it is best not to act on a fleeting feeling. I fell in love with a man who was not who (or what) he appeared to be. I stayed in an abusive marriage hoping that the ghost of the man he once was would come back to me.

Of course, when I met Gerald, I didn't see him for who he was. I'm not sure if *he* even knew what kind of man he really was. I'll never forget the day I met him, because, looking back, it was so ironic. I met him in church. I thought it was perfect, really. Who doesn't want to meet their Prince Charming while sitting in a church pew? What better place is there to find a life partner than at church? His family attended the same church I did, but I'd never met him before. He had been serving in the military when I started going to their church. It was five months after my heart was still reeling from my first heartbreak, that Gerald came back home to Florida.

That Sunday, he sat next to me in church. The thought never once crossed my mind that he would become my husband two short years later. In fact, I only knew he was interested in me when a mutual friend told me. It took me by surprise. I thought it was strange that he was interested in me. At the time, we were nothing more than strangers. How could he want to date me when he knew nothing about me? Over the next few months, he pursued me relentlessly. His persistence was flattering…but I didn't stop to consider that his keen focus on me and *only* me might not have been such a good thing after all.

When I finally gave in and let him have my phone number, my heart thought we were destined for each other. The more we talked, the more he seemed to say all the things I had been waiting for all my life. It seemed perfect. He seemed perfect.

I was young and naive. I fell for it. I went from thinking about who I was, and what I wanted to be, and what I hoped I would become, to only thinking about him. We started dating and we grew extremely close extremely fast. Things started to evolve, so we decided to make it official. He was so nice and sweet. He was everything I thought I wanted and we spent a lot of time together. I was in love…or at least I thought I was.

I told him everything. I was never shy to talk about my heart condition, never have been, and never will. I also knew there was no way I could hide it. I had a big scar on my chest from where I'd had open heart surgery, and it's not something that can easily be hidden. I told him all about my health and the surgeries and everything I had been through. I figured it was better to get it all out in the open now rather than later. We talked to his family about it, and while his mother was concerned that I was 'fragile,' he told me he was in it for the long haul, and that he was prepared to take care of me.

"I love you with health conditions or not." he'd tell me.

We started writing letters and talking on the phone constantly. We talked about our future. We shared our dreams, our passions, and our secrets. He told me about his family's history of abuse and how heavily it weighed on his heart. His relationship with his father was strained, and he hated the way his father treated his mother. He told me he never wanted to be like his father. He wanted to be a better man than his father. He spoke with such conviction, and it seemed like he believed what he was saying. He was so sure of himself, so sure that he would never turn out like his father. As he talked to me about everything he'd witnessed in his family, I felt my heart break for him. I was convinced that no one who had experienced that much pain could inflict that same kind of pain and hurt on others. I was wrong.

After he left the military things were rough for him. Because he couldn't get a stable job in Miami, he decided to move to California with his brother and sister-in-law. We were still dating, but I stayed behind in Miami. I think our long distance relationship helped hide his true nature, or at the very least, made it harder for me to see. I knew that most people might have advised against being in a long distance relationship with a military man, but I didn't care. I wanted to make it work, no matter the cost. It did put a strain on our relationship. It made things even more difficult for us, but in my eyes, it only helped prove the depth of our love for each other. If we could love each other that strongly from a distance, we would be able to love each other with the kind of fierceness I had only dreamed of once we were together again.

Through our telephone conversations, I started to see bits and pieces of the real him hiding underneath his uniform. He had issues, serious ones, but he promised he would change. I believed him, too. I wanted so badly to be loved as passionately and intensely as he seemed to love me. When I discovered that he was addicted to pornography, I was convinced I could rescue him. I honestly did believe that our love would be strong enough to curve his desires. After all, didn't true love always prevail over adversity in all the best romance novels? His addiction was something I was sure I could handle, something I could 'love away.'

I considered it a minor flaw we could overcome. If I could show him enough love and give him enough compassion, he wouldn't need to rely on pornography. Being with him was so easy and fun that I was willing to look past it and all the other warning signs that seemed to pop up more and more the longer we dated. Whenever he would lose his temper or have drastic mood swings, I made excuses for him.

*He's just having a bad day. Maybe he's depressed? I guess it could all be stress related. He's going through a lot right now….*

Whatever rationale I came up with, I knew we could make it through as long as we loved each other enough.

It was only a few months into our relationship when he told me he loved me. He said he couldn't live without me, and at that moment, I felt the same way. He made my heart feel things that I thought could only happen in the movies. He flew from California to Miami and proposed to me. We were so happy to tell everyone that we were planning our wedding, and I was thrilled to be engaged to the man I loved. I was so thrilled that it was all finally happening for me.

Things only got stormier the more we started planning our wedding. While his father and younger brother adored me, and couldn't wait for me to join their family, his mother was more negative. He began to digest her negativity, and in turn, that negativity started to affect me. The closer we got to our wedding date, the more stuff she put in his head. She said it was normal to interfere this much in her children's lives, but even though we were both 'island people,' I didn't know what she was talking about. My parents— strict as they were — didn't try to control every single aspect of our lives. When I met Gerald, they didn't try to pull us apart like his mother did. If I was happy, they were happy.

"You have an American mentality," his mother would tell me. "You think too much like the people here...you're not Haitian enough anymore."

The majority of Haitians are very controlling in general. If you allow them to, they'll control your life. Maybe I was Americanized, but I wasn't used to all the controlling and manipulating that seemed to be such a deep part of my new family-to-be's life. I wasn't willing to bow down to them. I had no intention of being pushed around. I fought back, and this made me different. My fiancé wanted me to mingle and blend in. He wanted me to be as close to his mother and sister as he was, but we never really were. I was close to his mother for a short period of time, but it didn't last long. The overstepping bothered me, and I felt disrespected. I'd frequently tell him that although his family was important to me, I was marrying *him...not* his family.

All the 'he said, she said' created a lot of unnecessary stress and tension, and we almost called it off, but I listened to my naive heart, and we proceeded with the engagement. It wasn't long after this period of doubt that we went through with the wedding.

# CHAPTER 12

## *The Truth About Marriage*

The day of my wedding arrived and I could not have been happier. Friends and family had gathered together to celebrate with us, and our church family helped with anything and everything we needed. Finally…the girl with the heart disease was getting her happy ending. Today there would be no pitying glances, or sympathetic looks directed toward Carline and her 'condition.' Today I was just Carline, and I was getting married.

The music started, and the double doors to the church swung open. My father walked up and took my arm. He patted my hand and held onto me tightly as we walked down the aisle toward my fiancé. When we finally reached the altar, I tried to take my arm back, but my father wouldn't let go.

"Dad? What are you doing?"

"I'm not ready to let you go yet." he said.

"Okay," I said, and started laughing. "It's time. Come on. Go sit down."

He shook his head. "No. He can't have you." he looked up at my fiancé. "You can't have her."

"Dad!" I started laughing so hard. "Dad, you need to go sit down. Go find a seat and sit down."

After more prodding, he eventually gave up on the joke and went to sit down next to my mother, and the pastor proceeded with the ceremony. We got through almost the entire service uninterrupted.

"If anyone knows why these two should not be joined together in holy matrimony, speak now or forever hold your peace."

My father, without skipping a beat, stood up. He smoothed the front of his tux, cleared his throat, and raised his hand.

"Yes, I object. I changed my mind. This is not going to happen."

"Dad!" I said, completely exasperated and trying not to laugh. "You need to find yourself a seat and sit down. Sit!"

The first few months of marriage were filled with absolute bliss. I was filled with all the joy newlyweds feel. At first, being married was like breathing in the cool, crisp mountain air on a bright fall morning. It made my lungs sting and brought tears to my eyes, but I loved every minute of it. I thought the thrill was what it meant to truly be alive. When the doctors had diagnosed me all those years ago, I had assumed feelings like love and passion and anything so vibrantly rich would forever be lost to me. Being married to my new husband opened my eyes. It made me realize that I could still live life in full color. I still had time to live a life full of joy and love and all those other wonderful life rites that I thought I would never get a chance to experience.

Soon after we were married, he took me back to California. We moved back in with his brother and his sister-in-law. Because I didn't know anyone in California, I was glad to have some family close by. Still, we were married now, and it was time to figure out precisely what it meant for two to become one flesh. Before getting married, I had fantasized about what it would be like. I looked forward to waking up every morning next to my best friend. I assumed that any trials or tribulations we encountered would be overshadowed by the love we had for one another.

Even though I thought I knew what it really meant to be married, I still didn't truly know. Marriage is a holy covenant that a man and woman enter in with God. It is not a covenant to be taken lightly. The weight of the responsibility a husband owes his wife, a wife to her husband, and both of them owe to God is sacred. It should never be entered into carelessly, and the true joys of marriage are often taken for granted.

Marriage is one of the beautiful ways that God grows both men and women. He matures us through the process of being in holy unity together. Life changes often, and nothing stays the same when we grow up; with age, we get a lot of responsibilities, and people start expecting things from you… things you weren't expected to do earlier in life. You have to learn to navigate the sacred space of compromise without losing who you are. The delicate balance of blending your lives together without trying to overpower one another is something that couples must continue to seek help from God. You have to learn how to not only *choose* love for your spouse, but also to choose love for your *spouse's family*. There is no way to separate your husband from his family. When you marry him, you marry them. This isn't something that most women are ready for, and it was something that I certainly wasn't prepared for.

When you have a healthy marriage, your spouse can help you navigate these waters more easily. You will challenge each other to grow, but you will also nourish and give each other strength. Your husband will love you as Christ loves the church. His love will be unconditional, sacrificial to the point of dying to his own sinful ways, and never-ending. A healthy marriage is a representation to the world of how Christ loves the church. It is an unwavering bond that personifies patience, understanding, extending grace, and forgiveness. This is why marriage can be easily complicated if your spouse is unequally yoked, or if he doesn't care for you more than he cares for his own selfish desires…your marriage will be far from what God intended it to be. No amount of unconditional love on your part will be able to make it whole. You will fight alone. I say this as a warning to those who think they can change a man or that their love is enough for them both. I've walked down that very path and fervently prayed that if I loved him enough, I could love us both, and keep us whole. The true reality of it is, the more you fight for someone who will never fight for you, the more you will be torn apart.

You will find that your best friend, the person you used to love to roll over and see every morning, is now your enemy. A sea of hurt and a mountain of distrust will separate you, and the bond you once had will be broken almost beyond repair. It is only God's intervention on your marriage that can fix it, and only then both spouses have to be willing to fall under God's authority and uphold His commands for our lives in order to completely heal the marriage. Even then, this healing process will take years.

Marriage changes your life, and you will never see things the same way again. It requires both individuals to change, and it is that change that will often reveal to us who a person really is and where their heart is at. Nobody is perfect, and no one is inherently bad. Marriage is the fire that will melt our imperfections, and it is up to us to choose whether or not to grow toward God's plan for our purification, or fight and hold onto the desires of our flesh.

For me, the weight of my marriage changed my priorities and routines. I went from being a carefree girl one day, to a responsible woman who had a desire to put her spouse's wants and needs above her own. My husband was affected by the weight of our marriage differently. Perhaps if I had heeded the warning signs, the history of abuse in his family, or the problems he confessed to struggling with, my marriage would have played out differently, but I didn't. Now, my marriage serves as a warning for others. A warning that just because your heart tells you that you love someone, doesn't mean you have to put yourself at risk.

# CHAPTER 13

## *Explosions*

While Gerald's late father and brother adored me, his mother was not fond of me. They were raised very differently than I was, and their attitude was often negative, and I felt uncomfortable when I was around them. They could be bossy and demeaning, and I just didn't fit in with them. I should have known that problems would arise when my mother-in-law first started budging into my marriage.

Gerald was a momma's boy, and he'd do anything he could to please her. It wasn't long before she was making decisions for him and calling the shots in our marriage. She'd berate me if I didn't do things exactly the way she wanted, and she made it very clear how she felt about me. She was my mother-in-law, and I wanted to be respectful, but Gerald started telling her things that she had no business knowing. There are some things that should stay between a husband and wife, but Gerald told his mother deeply personal things that never should have been shared with anyone but me and him.

Things slowly declined, and while a large portion of it had to do with his mother's complete lack of boundaries, Gerald's baggage caught up with him. And it wasn't long before the ideal picture of how I wanted my marriage to be was shattered. The verbal abuse turned physical, and it all changed the day he pushed me. It wasn't a playful jostle or a nudge. There was no love in his eyes, and even now, I can still see them full of anger. It was so foreign to any emotion I'd ever seen in him. Even before his rage had physically manifested itself, I was unhappy in our marriage. His constant criticism, intimidation, and demands forced me to spend my every waking second dedicated to making him happy. He thought it was my life's purpose to revolve around making him happy. I couldn't do things for myself or anything that would risk his happiness.

I eventually stood up to my mother-in-law, but it took me a long time to stand up to Gerald. That wouldn't happen for another couple of years, but I did put my foot down with his mother. She was yelling at me one day, and spewing negative things. She was yelling at me like I was one of her children, and I'd finally had enough.

"Listen," I began calmly. "I'm not your child, so you don't get to yell at me. You don't get to do that. I'm a grown woman, and you don't get to tell me what to do. If you want to yell at someone, yell at your own kids, but don't yell at me."

She wasn't happy, but I didn't care. There was absolutely no reason she should speak to me that way. I walked away, and after I did, my brother-in-law pulled me aside.

"Good job, Carline." he said. "Don't let her talk to you that way. Good for you for standing up to her. I'm proud of you."

# CHAPTER 14

*Unexpected News*

My husband and I had been married for three months, and things didn't seem to be getting any better. I struggled to meet his needs, and he struggled to love me the way a wife deserves to be loved. But I tried. I tried my best to be enough for him. When things were going good, we were happy. I could see the man I fell in love with, and I could tell myself that the angry, violent, selfish creature was going away. I told myself he was changing for me. I was wrong, of course, but I didn't know that. I so desperately wanted to be happy with him that I saw every little improvement as a step in the right direction. I wasn't sure what could ease the strain between us, but I hoped for the best.

It was around this time when I began feeling sick at work. I prepared myself for the worst. I assumed that my sickness was connected to my heart medication, and dread filled me. Even though I had always known it was a possibility, I didn't want to deal with trying to balance my heart disease with my struggling marriage, but my body had other plans.

I worked in an office separated only by glass, from top to bottom. I had no door or wall I could hide behind. So when I put my head down on my desk, and tried to catch my breath, one of my co-workers knocked on the door. I heard her voice float in from the hall.

"Carline? Carline, sweetie…are you okay?"

I shook my head without lifting it from the desk, but I didn't want her to worry, so I told her I was fine. It was probably nothing, and I'd feel better in a little bit. I felt like I was zoning in and out of focus. My ears rang and echoed and the world around me seemed to blur, and I felt this painful pressure…but I didn't tell my co-worker that.

Luckily, she didn't believe me, and she called Gerald. He picked me up and took me to the hospital. As soon as I was in the ER the doctors began their usual line of questions.

"Are you on any medications?"

"I take *Coumadin* for my heart."

"Is there any chance you could be pregnant?"

"No, I can't have children."

"Do you consume any alcohol or tobacco products?"

"No. I don't."

I prayed that I was wrong about my heart medication causing me to be sick. I felt like my marriage didn't need any further complications, and I couldn't handle any more heart trouble. Little did I know just how far off I was about the cause of my sickness.

He stood by me while the doctor took some routine blood samples and returned twenty or thirty minutes later. The doctor walked into the room. He closed the door behind him and sat on his swivel chair. He looked at my charts once more.

"Is it the *Coumadin*? Should I be put on a new medication?" I asked.

He shook his head. "No, no. Nothing like that. Actually, I wanted to tell you congratulations."

"Congratulations?" I repeated. I could not have been more confused. "Congratulations? For what?"

"You're pregnant, Carline."

My husband was thrilled. He jumped for joy at the news that he was going to be a father, while I felt like the world had come tumbling down around me. The words of my doctors echoed in my mind as I recalled the prognosis they had given me as a teenager. If I had a baby, it would kill me or the baby…or even both of us. What should have been the happiest news of my life was tainted by the dark stain of my heart disease.

"I'm pregnant?"

"Yes." he said. "Due to your RHD, you're considered an extremely high-risk case. For every second that the fetus grows inside you, you'll be risking not only your own life, but your baby's life as well."

Once again, it felt like my heart condition was robbing me of something that came so easily to other people. At that moment, it was like the doctor could read my mind. He began to inform us of all the risks we would be taking if we decided to continue with the pregnancy.

Gerald's face fell. He and the doctor began discussing all of the outcomes, and I felt too shaken with grief to truly process it all. I never imagined I would get pregnant, but now that I was, what was the right choice? God makes it very clear in His word that murder is a sin and that He has knitted us together in our mother's womb before she even knows we are there. I knew there was a plan for the life that grew inside me, but I feared that developing that little miracle full term would cost me my life.

As these questions rampaged in my head, the door to the hospital room burst open, and two more doctors entered. My husband and I were shocked that they, too, were saying the best decision for my health was to abort the baby. Tears flowed freely from my eyes as I considered their words.

"I know this is a difficult time for you." one of the other doctors began. "It can be a lot to take in. We're here to answer any questions that you might have."

The female doctor took another look at my chart and stepped up. She met my eyes and repeated the same information that the first doctor had told me.

"It's better that we perform the abortion as quickly as possible. I can have one of the nurses put together some information on the routine for you and we can get you on the schedule as soon as next week, okay?"

She said it so matter-of-factly…as if there was no other possible course of action that we could take. I said nothing, but looked at the doctors. I inhaled, and it probably appeared as though I was processing what they were saying, or that I was still in shock.

"Carline? You doing okay there?"

"Yes…and I understand what you're saying—"

"Good." she said. "So I'll just talk to Stacy at the front desk and tell her that—"

"I'm not killing my baby."

She stopped, like she couldn't believe what I just said.

"I'm sorry, what?"

"I heard what you said," I continued. "And I don't believe in abortion. I'm not going to murder my child."

The doctors looked stunned. They looked at me like I was stupid.

"Okay, let me say this a different way…" the female doctor said. "If you go through with this pregnancy…."

"I know." I said. "I understand, really, I do. I've had this disease for a very long time. This is nothing new for me. I understand what you're saying, but abortion is not an option for us."

The male doctors scratched their heads. The female doctor blinked. She bent down and stared at me like I was a child who didn't understand.

"Listen, lady…do you not care about your life? You *will* die if you go through with this."

"I heard you."

"Best case scenario your baby will have *Down syndrome*…not *maybe* have Down syndrome, there is no world in which you might have a *normal* term baby, you will *not* have a normal baby. That's *not* in the cards for you."

"Uh-huh."

"Look, is it a religion thing? I don't think God would want you to die so that you can maybe have an abnormal child. Don't you think that doesn't seem like something He wouldn't expect from you? I think He would make an exception for you, in a case like this, don't you?"

"I'm keeping my baby."

We went around and around for what seemed like forever before they finally gave up on me. One thing was clear; they thought I was crazy, but no amount of arguing was going to change my mind. They switched my daily medication from *Coumadin* to shots of *Heparin*. Both medications were blood thinners, but the difference was that the *Coumadin* was stronger, and overall, much better for my heart. While the *Heparin* was a weaker medication, it was better for the baby. Switching my medications made me uneasy, but I was willing to do what I had to for my child.

The moment I found out I was pregnant, I became a mother. Something in me changed, and I no longer considered what was in the best interest for me or my husband. I focused on what was in the best interest of our unborn child. He didn't have a voice for himself yet, but I knew in my heart that God called me to advocate for him. It was my right as his mother to look after him.

Before we left, we scheduled our first visit with the high-risk OBGYN who worked at the same hospital. The car ride home was charged with silent tension. Neither of us spoke about what the doctors said, or the situation we now found ourselves in. I wondered what my husband thought.

*Would he be willing to risk my life and the life of our child for me to stand firm in our faith? Was I?*

When we got inside the house we finally started to discuss it. I was relieved to discover he and I felt the same way. But later that week, the night before our appointment with the specialist, he and I got into an argument, and he stayed up very late drinking. Until this incident, I didn't know that he drank. I brushed it aside, steeling myself to focus on the next day. At our follow-up appointment, I was prepared for the likelihood that the doctor would try to discourage us from continuing with the pregnancy. When it inevitably happened, I locked eyes with the doctor and explained that we would not be aborting our child. I explained to them that God placed the baby in my womb, He would deliver the baby safe and sound. This doctor, too, tried to dissuade me, but like the others, he eventually gave up.

Even though I put my trust in the Lord for the safety of my pregnancy, I did worry about the high chance that my blood thinners would cause my child to be born with a genetic disorder. It's not that I was afraid my love would change for my child if he or she was going to be born with Special needs. It wasn't that at all. I knew in my heart that I would love my child no matter what. I would love my baby with everything I had in me. The anxiety and fear I felt in regard to the pregnancy was rooted in my deep desire to protect my child. I didn't want my medication to affect them in a way that would make their life more difficult. I was so concerned for my unborn child, I didn't even care if it meant risking my own life in return for the safety of theirs.

Once they switched me from the *Coumadin* to the *Heparin*, they put me on close supervision. It was still a blood thinner, but it was safer for pregnant women; albeit less effective for my heart condition. During my pregnancy, I leaned closer to God for His provision, and I could feel my walk with Him strengthen. My friends, family, and church family began praying fervently for my healing. As my baby grew, I could feel God's hand of protection around us both.

The further along in my pregnancy I got, the more my husband and I fought. I noticed that he would drink for longer and longer sessions. It was then that I realized he was an alcoholic, and my prayers to God changed to include safekeeping for our child…not only while I carried him in my body, but when I carried him in this world as well.

# CHAPTER 15

*Walking On Eggshells*

During what should have been my honeymoon period, I did not do what most women did. I didn't gush about how much I loved my husband and how we lived in marital bliss. Instead, I unknowingly began a pattern I would carry on for years. I hid the nature of my relationship from my friends, family, and as a result, I silently suffered because I was too ashamed to ask anyone for help. I never breathed a word to anyone. Not even my brother-in-law and his wife, and we shared a home. I was consumed with guilt, and no matter what he did, I still protected him. I assumed that it was my own fault— I had married someone as cruel as him and now I had to suffer alone. Who was I to complain when I had caused my own suffering?

I didn't realize that these thoughts were from the devil. No matter the degree of abuse in your relationship, it is never your fault! You never deserve it. God is never punishing you. He loves you as you are and sent His son to pay the price for you. He would never harm you, and He does not condone others to hurt His children. It took me years to reach this understanding.

The morning after our first prenatal appointment, my husband and I got into the worst argument that we had in our marriage up until that point. The argument grew heated quickly. I can still hear the echoes of our fighting bouncing around in my head. It was like we were bringing out the worst in each other, and at that moment, I didn't recognize either one of us. Suddenly, he jumped up with panther speed and grabbed me by the neck. His eyes were washed over with uncontrollable rage. His hands clamped down around my neck.

"I'm going to break your neck!" he hissed.

As the air ran out of my lungs, a horrible stillness flooded my mind. I know I struggled, but even while my body fought for breath, my mind tried to console me. I was a few weeks pregnant and states away from my family. No one could help me. Even though his younger brother and his brother's wife lived with us, they were at work. I was trapped alone with the monster I called 'my husband.'

I started shaking uncontrollably. I knew that I needed to make him let me go. I couldn't breathe, and I worried that our child might be struggling for life just as I was. Panic exploded through me like sudden bombs, and my mind began to race. I needed air. I needed him to let me go. I needed help. In barely a whisper, I told him that if he didn't let me go, I would call the police. I'm not sure if that desperate threat was what snapped him out of his rage, or if it was the feeling of his hands crushing my windpipe, but he released me after I threatened to call the cops. The moment I was free from his grip, I ran to the bathroom, locked the door, and called the police.

I could hear him prowling around the apartment, while I waited, crying and gasping for breath. He was a wild animal, and he said that it was my fault. It was always my fault, and in the few short months we had been married, I had already started to believe him. When the police arrived to arrest him and press charges, I wasn't sure what to do. A small voice urged me to let them take him. There were bruises in the shape of fingerprints on both my arms and neck. He deserved to go to jail for what he did. But that voice was drowned out by another voice. This new voice told me that it would not have happened if I hadn't aggravated him as much as I did.

*Could I really betray the trust of the man I loved? The one who said he loved me back?*

111

I was afraid. Afraid of my husband, afraid for my baby, and afraid of what pressing charges against him would mean for the rest of his life. I was afraid that if I said anything, he'd stay in prison, and I didn't want to live with the thought that I was the one who put him there. When they started to handcuff him, I begged for them to stop. I told them we'd only had a minor disagreement. I pleaded with them to let him go. I begged them not to arrest him.

The officers knew I was lying, and I knew that they knew I wasn't telling the truth. My husband agreed that it was nothing. They didn't remove the handcuffs. Instead, they pulled me aside and explained that they had heard my call to dispatch. They heard the desperate fear in my voice that exposed the truth of the danger I was in. I explained it all away and made excuses for my husband, like I always did. They looked at me, doing their best to convince me that it was okay, that he could go to jail and that nobody would hold me accountable. I told them it was fine, and that they should go. I don't know if the look in their eyes was pity, but as they left, I pitied myself.

"Okay, ma'am…but if you ever call us again, we'll arrest him. Be careful, ma'am. Have a good day."

I had bound myself to a man who was nothing like the man I had dated. I truly believe that when he first threatened to kill me, if someone else had stepped in to encourage me to leave him, I might have listened. I might have believed someone if they insisted that I wasn't wrong for being afraid. Maybe I would have been able to see that it wasn't my fault. Maybe I just needed someone else to say it first. But no one knew, and no one came to my side. When his family eventually found out about what happened between us, and that I had called the cops, they looked at me like *I* was the monster because *I* had gotten him arrested.

So, instead of sharing what had happened with my family, I took on the misbelief that I was the root of all of our problems. I believed that it was my fault, and if I could only be a good enough wife to him, then my marriage would be everything I dreamed it would be. Unfortunately, the struggles in my marriage went from bad to worse. His anger and resentment toward me built while I was pregnant and he became even more verbally abusive. With every negative comment directed toward me, it became harder for me to get through the daily criticisms. I began to view myself as worthless. I was so unhappy that I actually couldn't sleep and I couldn't find the desire to eat. I was so wracked with guilt that it became difficult for me to function.

I steadily began to lose weight during my pregnancy. I tried to find the joy in carrying my child, but it was all too often overshadowed by the fear I felt for my life. Every morning I constantly wondered if that day would be the day my husband carried out his threat and killed me, or if my pregnancy would kill me first. The constant fear for my life

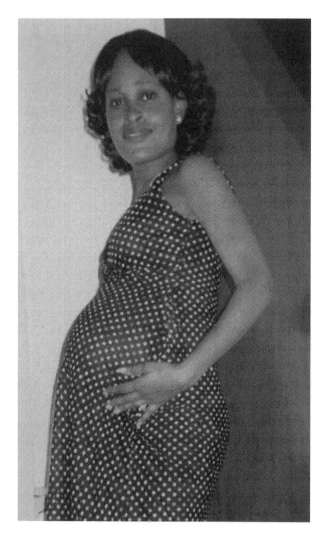

*Carline's pregnancy with her first child*

was crushing. When I was five months pregnant, I went for my routine ultrasound appointment and was reminded how much my pregnancy was putting my life at risk. After taking a look at my beautiful baby boy on the ultrasound, my gynecologist told me they were left with no choice but to abort the baby. I was informed that there was still no guarantee that the baby would be able to be carried full term, and that the risk to my life was simply not worth it. As I left the room, I felt like my world was crashing down around me. There was no hope left. How could there be when even the doctors were telling me to give up?

I laid down on the couch in the lobby of the hospital and waited for my husband to pick me up. I put my hand on my stomach and felt the life within me stirring. Tears threatened to spill down my face, and I wondered where God was.

A vision overcame me: an elderly man with pearl white hair. He came up to me and asked, "Why are you so unhappy, my daughter? Do not be afraid, the child you are carrying is fine, he will bring you joy. He will make you very happy."

I tried to explain to him all of my doubts and fears, but he merely smiled at me. In my vision, the man gently laid his hand on my forehead and then told me, "All is well." Then he disappeared. When the vision cleared, I realized it was an angel of the Lord who had visited me and brought me comfort. I kept this experience close to my heart and let it wrap me in strength. I wasn't sure what would ultimately happen in my pregnancy, but after that day, I felt renewed. I regained my strength and I did not fear the unknown any longer.

# CHAPTER 16

## *Answered Prayers*

I wasn't sure how long my newfound sense of peace would last. When I was six months pregnant, that peace came with me when I was hospitalized for being underweight. I thought it was ironic that the complications that were arising now were not from my heart condition, but were from the circumstances and condition of my marriage. I was six months pregnant and eighty-six pounds. My doctors informed me that being as underweight as I was was actually putting my baby in more danger. They kept me in the hospital for a week. They consistently and constantly monitored the vitals of my child and me. While I was there, I realized that the distance between my husband and I was giving me the space I needed to take care of myself. I was no longer continually being put down by him. Even though we saw each other while I was hospitalized, I was still guaranteed some space away from him, and I started to feel like myself for the first time in a long time.

When I was discharged, I knew what I needed to do. I called my parents and asked if I could come home to Florida. At first I told them I was homesick, but the longer we were on the phone, the real issues started coming to light. When I explained to them that I was miserable, and that my baby wasn't growing like he needed to, my parents immediately helped me make arrangements to fly home.

"You're coming back home on the next flight." my father told me. "You're going to give birth in Miami. Your husband is not being responsible. You'll come back home and you'll have the baby here."

They got my ticket immediately, and as much as I wanted to run away and never look back, I couldn't. I was living in San Diego county in the city of Vista at the time, and my flight had been booked through Los Angeles International Airport. The drive was just under a hundred miles and took anywhere from an hour and a half to upwards of three hours. I could have taken a taxi, but taxies were expensive, and I knew that I wouldn't feel (and probably wouldn't be) safe as a pregnant woman in a two hour long taxi cab ride to the airport. Even though I was scared of my husband, I still would have felt safer driving with him than I would have with a complete stranger.

It was three days later, and we hadn't really spoken since our last fight, we were just sort of cohabitating. I wanted to avoid him altogether, and I would have, but I needed a ride. When I finally asked him for one, he told me that he wasn't going to give me a ride, and that if I wanted to go, I'd have to figure out a way to get to the airport myself.

"Really?" I asked him. "You're not even going to give me a ride to the airport?"

He shook his head.

"No. Find a ride or don't go."

I called my parents and told them that he refused to take me. I could tell my father was irritated.

"Hang up, I'll call him." he told me.

I hung up, and Gerald's phone started to ring. He picked it up and answered like it was the most normal thing in the world.

"Hello?"

"Listen, if something happens to my daughter, I'm holding you responsible. You're her husband. Take her to the airport."

I could hear my father's stern voice on the other end of the phone. Gerald said okay, hung up the phone, and stood up.

He came back with the car keys. We loaded my suitcase into the trunk, and got into the car, and my husband drove me the two hours to LAX airport.

My parents welcomed me home with open arms, and as soon as I saw them, I fell into their arms. It was such a relief to be home and away from my husband. On the flight from California to Florida, I had considered staying in Florida and never going back to my husband, and when my parents held me in their arms in the Florida airport, I had every intention of doing just that. I wasn't going to go back to him. Ever.

My parents were shocked to see the condition I was in. My mother held me in her arms and cried. I knew they had been worrying about me, and seeing me in person hadn't made it any better. They asked me so many questions about why I was so skinny, and what the actual reason was for me coming home. I managed to brush off the majority of their questions.

"You look totally different, Carline." my mother told me as we got in the car to leave the airport. "You are now even smaller than you were before."

When we reached my parent's house, my father went inside. My mother told me to wait. Once my father was inside, she turned to me. She didn't say anything for a long time. She just looked at me.

"What is it?" I asked.

"Carline," she said. "I don't want to get in your business, but you are my daughter and I want to know if you are okay. So I'm asking you, are you okay?"

"I don't want to discuss my marriage."

"I know, Carline, I know." she said. "You've always been a very private person, but I need to know if you are okay."

I nodded, and I told her the same thing I'd told her before I got on the plane; I was miserable, I was tired, and I was unhappy. I did finally tell her that Gerald was verbally abusive, but I never said anything about being physically abused. It didn't feel right to tell my parents, and I knew that once I told my family about what my husband was doing to me, there'd be no stopping my dad and brothers from giving my husband a taste of his own medicine.

I stayed with my parents for about two to two and a half months. After the first couple of weeks, my husband called me every day— crying— for the next two months. He would tell me how much he missed me, how much he was going to change for me, and how he wanted to be an amazing father to our baby. He told me that he wanted to put the past behind us and start over. At first, I could still feel the sting of all of his abusive words and the fear of his threats, and I had no interest in going back to him. But little by little, he wore me down. We had a history, him and I. He was once again the man I loved, sweet, caring, and willing to do anything for me. I could still imagine the person I had fallen in love with hiding somewhere inside of him. He had to be in there. I couldn't have fallen in love with a wolf masquerading in sheep's clothing! Surely some part of the man I loved was just waiting to come back to me, and being away from me had provided him with the clarity he needed.

The more we talked, the more confused I felt. I didn't want my child to grow up fatherless, and my husband really did seem like a different man. I had convinced myself that the distance and time apart had helped him change. So, when he called me and begged me to come home to him because he wanted to be there for the birth of our son and wouldn't be able to go to Florida, I agreed to go back. My parents were opposed to the idea, of course, but I insisted. I told them that he was my husband, after all. When they drove me to the hospital, I could see the hope in their eyes that my life would be better now, and I carried that same hope. I wanted a better life for us, together, as a family. Over the next month, until our son was born, my husband showered me with reassurances that he was different, and against my better judgment, I believed him.

To his credit, he did a wonderful job of pretending he had changed. During the last month of my pregnancy, I honestly believed that he had amended his violent and abusive ways. I was ready to bring our son into the world with a loving, stable, two-parent home. I still remember eagerly waking up two weeks after my last check-up and thinking that today could be the day I would go into labor. Everything we had fought for with the doctors would come to a head today. I would either end this experience holding my baby boy, or I would finish it being held by the Lord.

Despite the excitement and anticipation we felt for our son's birth, we still didn't have a name picked out. Every name my husband picked out, I hated. He wanted to name our child after one of his family members. He didn't care if it was his sister or his cousin or his uncle…he just wanted to give our son a "family name."

"Forget it." I told him. "Just forget it. Let's just call him baby."

"But…" he started.

"If I hear one of your family member's names one more time…"

"But Carline…"

"Listen," I said. "Why would we name our child after one of your family members?"

"To honor them." he said, as if it was the most normal thing in the world. "I want to name our son after my family."

"Name him after your family?"

"Yes." he said.

"Why would we name them after your family? Your sister has kids. Your brother has kids…and they didn't even name their own kids after themselves, so why would *we* name *our* child after *them* if *they* didn't even name *their child* after *them*?"

"Uhhhh…."

"Exactly." I said, and turned on my heel. I thought the argument was over and we'd look for new baby names together. My husband followed after me, not as ready to move onto new name ideas.

"Can we at least name him Gerald?"

"After you and your dad?"

He nodded.

"Sure. Then we'd have Gerald the third. It'd make my dad happy if we named the baby after him."

I sighed. "But your dad doesn't even go by Gerald, he goes by Gerry."

"So?"

"You don't even like your name."

"So?"

"So why would I give my son his father's name if both his father *and* his grandfather don't even go by that name? Huh? Why would I do that?"

A few days after we had that conversation, he approached me, and told me he had an idea for a name for the baby. I sat down, and waited to hear him out.

"As long as it's not a family name." I said.

"It's not."

"Okay, good." I said.

He went on.

"I was thinking about it a lot, and I was thinking… what if we did both our names?"

"…both our names?"

"Yes." he continued. "Both our names. Listen, the first letters of my name are 'Ge,' right?"

I nodded.

"And the first couple letters of your name are 'Car,' right?"

"Uh-huh."

"So let's put them together!" he said, excitedly. "Let's name our son Gecar. What do you think about that name?"

I thought about it.

"Hmmm. Gecar…okay, yeah, okay."

"Great!"

"But I have one condition." I said.

He nodded and waited for me to finish.

"With two 'r's….we spell it 'G-e-c-a-r-r. Gecarr. Two 'r's. That makes it more unique and special."

And that was how we picked the name for our son: Gecarr.

When the day finally came for Gecarr to be born, we arrived at the hospital and they proceeded to get vital signs on our son. They told us that his heartbeat was too low, and he must be having difficulty breathing. Immediately, they told us they would need to do an emergency-cesarean. I tried to remain calm as they informed us that there was a high probability that once they started the surgery, all the years of my blood thinners would take full effect, and I would bleed to death.

I remembered the vision that God had given me earlier on in the pregnancy. I held onto the truth that God had a plan for all of this. He would use this experience to bring Him glory. I was afraid that they were going to take me to the operating table right away, but luckily they told me they had to wait twelve hours before I could have a c-section. I insisted that I wanted to have a natural birth. I knew the risks that we were taking, but I also knew that God would protect me and provide for me every step of the way as He had the entire pregnancy.

As soon as I was induced at zero centimeters, I started to feel my contractions. I was prepared for the fact that they would come in waves, but what I didn't realize is that it would be so painful. I started begging for an epidural, and the nineteen-hour labor that followed was the most hectic, painful, back-breaking agony of all my life. Finally, it was time to push the baby out.

When I was in position, my knees practically touching my cheeks, I heard the doctor telling me to push. I fought to push my baby. I pushed and I pushed until I couldn't push anymore. I heard the nurses and my husband say, "I see his head." Right then, I reached the point where I felt so tired that I was sure I wouldn't be able to finish. I became weak and tired, and the labor stopped progressing. Thankfully, the doctor used a soft cup with a handle and a vacuum pump to assist me with the last leg of delivery.

"Here you go, Carline. Here's your son."

The doctor handed me my baby. I was scared when I first saw him; I didn't realize that the suction would leave his head in a rounded cone shape.

"Doctor!" I said. "What's wrong with the top of his head?!"

She laughed as she told me, "Don't worry, Carline. It's from the vacuum. Lots of babies have cone-heads for a little while after birth. Don't worry, it'll go down. His head will be perfectly round and normal in a day or two. I promise."

My oldest son, Gecarr Giovanni Pierre, was born a healthy six pounds and one ounce. I remember holding my son in my arms and gazing down at his beautiful face. I fell in love with him from the moment I laid eyes on him. Instantly, I forgot about the pain and everything that I had endured in the last nine months. Looking back, I would do it all again as long as it meant that I could have the joy of being his mother. The angel from my vision was right, he brought me joy, unlike anything I had experienced thus far in life.

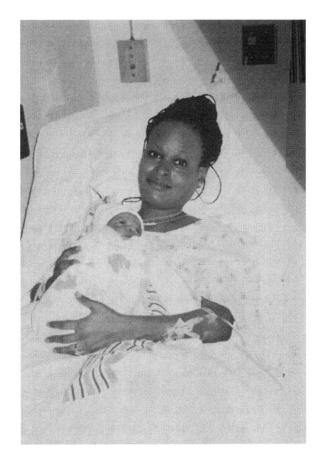

*Carline and baby Gecarr*

## CHAPTER 17

*Runaway Train*

The first three months of my son's life were a haze of motherhood bliss. I loved him unlike I had ever loved anyone before. It was holding him, feeding him, and showering him with love and affection that reminded me of God's love for His children. I couldn't help but wonder…if I loved my son this much, how much more did God love us to sacrifice His one and only son on the cross for our sins? Our little bundle of joy brought a change to our home, and he changed the way I viewed life.

I'm not sure if his presence gave me something to focus on other than my husband's criticisms, or if my husband was just as in love with our boy as I was— that he simply didn't have time to find things that were wrong with me.

Regardless, during this time, I was happy. Not long after Gecarr was born, Gerald's brother purchased a house in Georgia, and he and his wife invited us to go with them. We agreed, and moved to Georgia with them. Despite all the recent change, we were settling into our new home and our new family dynamic well. The adjustment, the lack of sleep, exhaustion, and an overabundance of love for the bundle of joy named Gecarr left me feeling content. I was thankful that God had allowed me to experience the joys of motherhood despite my health.

My son was a chance at the dream I had always wanted; he was a dream come true. I was sure that it was God who had granted me one child, but what I didn't know was that God would bless me with another baby boy. One morning, soon after we moved, I woke up with severe stomach pain. At first, I dismissed it. I had recently had a baby through natural delivery, and figured it was due to that. My body was changing, my hormones were running rampant as they adjusted to my son post-birth, and nursing him was leaving me constantly feeling hungry and drained. There was too much to take into consideration to be concerned that something was actually wrong with me.

Anytime one of my family members has something wrong with them, we drink tea. Perhaps it's an island thing, but we drink tea as an everyday remedy for a long list of ailments. My sister-in-law told me that I was probably just experiencing severe gas. I told her it didn't feel like gas. She shrugged and told me she'd make me a cup of tea. She did, and no matter how many cups of tea I drank, the pains remained the same.

My symptoms persisted and grew in intensity. I tried to convince myself that I was overreacting. They were only premenstrual cramps after all, and the reason it felt different was because it was my third period after having a baby. I wanted to tell myself all kinds of things to keep me from giving in to the pain, but finally, I couldn't take it anymore. I told my husband, and he rushed me to the nearest emergency room. As I clutched my stomach and informed them of my medical history, I tried my best to remain calm. My mind wanted me to drift to the worst-case scenarios, but my soul wanted me to focus on the tangible presence of God. I could feel Him sending me the calm I so desperately needed. God had provided for me so far, and He would continue to provide for me.

I tried my best to remain calm, waiting for them to tell me something was wrong with my medication, but what they told me instead was just as shocking as the first time I had heard it. I was pregnant again! My mind almost couldn't comprehend the news. I never expected to be pregnant again! I knew my son was my miracle from God. Here the Lord was, once again providing for me.

*Gecarr (9 months old)*

This time the news mixed my gratitude with my anxiety. The doctors informed us that I was four weeks pregnant, but because my pregnancies were so close together, this second pregnancy would be even harder on my body than my first pregnancy. They were more aggressive this time with their insistence that I terminate the pregnancy. They explained that my body hadn't had the proper time to recover; there was a much lower chance at having a viable full-term pregnancy, let alone a natural delivery.

I was scared, especially when we went to see our new high-risk OBGYN, and he was concerned, too. However, I knew that my second child was just as much of a miracle child as my first. God had blessed me with both of them, and nothing could convince me to end my son's life by having an abortion. We told the doctor that we had decided to carry on with the pregnancy and rely on our faith in God once again. He had made a way when there was none before, and we began to call on His name to do it again.

We drove back home. We hadn't spoken much on the ride back, but I didn't think anything of it. When we stepped out of the car and walked toward the house, I mentioned something about the visit with the specialist. It must have been about the doctor's recommendation to abort the baby, because my husband looked up at me and said the words I never thought I'd hear him say.

"I think he's right."

"Right? Right about what?"

He took the keys out of his pocket and opened the front door. He walked in, and I followed behind him and shut the door. He tossed the keys on the counter.

"About the abortion."

I froze.

"He's…right about the…abortion?"

"Yeah." he said, and nodded. "I think we should do it. It'd be stupid to go through all this again, Carline. Just get the abortion and be done with it. We don't need any more kids."

I couldn't believe what I was hearing. I had just assumed we would be on the same page. I mean, why wouldn't we be? But we weren't, and the entire thing turned into a huge fight. I thought that my own husband would be on my side, but he wasn't. I didn't care. No one could convince me to get rid of my baby…not even my husband.

# CHAPTER 18

## *Slow Motion*

The first six months of my pregnancy was filled with trying to balance the growing panic of the possibilities of complications and also trying to remain faithful to God's enduring promise. God had already taken care of me through one pregnancy, and I knew He would take care of me through this second one. But this pregnancy was much different than my first one. Getting pregnant when Gecarr was only three months old made it more difficult for me to care for myself, my son, and my husband.

The doctors had once again taken me off the *Coumadin* and put me back on the *Heparin*. But by the time I was six months pregnant, I'd started showing signs of many more complications than I had with the previous pregnancy. I started feeling chest pains and had difficulty breathing. I started throwing up blood. I asked my husband to take me to the emergency room, but he didn't want to take me. Not only was I sick, but the abuse was getting worse. I was in bad shape. Luckily, someone eventually convinced him that he should take me to the hospital.

Gerald drove me to the nearest twenty-four hour hospital in Powder Springs, Georgia. Bad news started flooding in as soon as we stepped inside the hospital. We were told that my mitral valve— a mechanical valve from my last surgery that was supposed to last forever— was clotted, I had pneumonia, and the baby was not breathing. My heart came to a thundering stop. I wondered how so much could go so wrong so quickly. The doctors did not hesitate. They told us that they needed to perform a c-section to deliver my son and then I would go into heart surgery right away.

I blanched. I was only six months pregnant, they couldn't do a c-section yet! It was too early. What would happen to him if they took him from my womb this early? What would happen to me? Out of nowhere, I was suddenly going to have two back to back surgeries and I had no time to mentally and emotionally prepare. I felt completely hopeless. I thought I was dreaming because reality seemed unreal. It was completely overwhelming, and I didn't know what to do or how to feel. I wanted to run back home, but I couldn't. I had to face what was happening to me.

A doctor walked in with a shot and explained that they were going to try to open the valve temporarily in order to deliver the baby, however; the shot would most likely cause the baby brain damage. Tears rolled down my cheeks as they explained to us that the baby was not a priority, I was. They would do everything they could to save me instead of the baby. Because of the state the baby was in, they were afraid that he was not going to make it. The news hit me like a blow to the stomach, gut-wrenching, and choking the will to live right out of me. I knew that even though I desperately wanted to give up amid my storm, I couldn't let the waters overtake me. It felt like the world, and everything in it was going in slow motion. I wanted to faint, but I couldn't because if I gave up, the baby would die. I was still fighting for both of our lives.

"Please," I begged. "Please…if it comes down to it, save my baby."

The doctor shook his head.

"We're trying to save *you*, not the baby."

The hospital quickly packed me up and rushed me by ambulance to Emory Hospital. Emory was a more equipped hospital in Atlanta, Georgia, where they were going to perform my second valve-replacement, lung surgery, and an emergency Cesarean. I thought I was dreaming. Then the enormity of what was happening slammed into me. I started shaking, and it became even more challenging to breathe. At that moment, I was struggling to make sense of what was happening, but looking back, I now know that my real struggle was accepting the truth that I was about to die.

I learned that day that you can't look backward, even if you know you are about to die. I had nothing to do except sit and wait, enjoy my physical pain, and after a while, realized that the only thing that mattered, were the people who are left behind. That day, my biggest concerns were for my first child, Gecarr, who was only ten months old, and my unborn child, Isaiah. I hoped and prayed that he would make it out of the surgery alive. I was not as sad for myself as I was for the ones I loved. I worried about my family. My health problems, which I had always known would lead to my eventual death, would fill them with deep sorrow. I cared more about them and the pain they would feel than I did thinking about all the things I would not live to see or enjoy. I came to the conclusion that the worst would be that I couldn't say goodbye, and that I would not see them again in this life.

I realized that once again, I did not want to die. The last time I had experienced this feeling, I came to terms with how beautiful my life was, even if it looked differently than the way I had always planned. But this time, the thing that would kill me wasn't of my own doing. The hard lesson I learned that day is that when death does come, it is very much out of our hands. As I wrestled with this, I slowly began to accept the inevitability of death.

I prayed and repented from my sins. I had no choice but to forgive everyone that wronged me. I forgave myself, and I accepted the fact that I probably wasn't going to make it. I didn't want to die, but I was ready to die— to be freed from stress, pain, and anguish. Salvation is available to any sinner right up to the point of death, but not all dying people have an opportunity to repent. Not everyone has adequate warning that death is ahead.

2 Corinthians 7:10 teaches us, "Godly sorrow brings repentance that leads to salvation and leaves no regret, but worldly sorrow brings death."

A repentant person doesn't blame God and others for his problems, he admits his own guilt and sin. Salvation is always received through repentance and faith in Jesus Christ. By all means, make sure that you do not presume God's grace by putting off repentance and faith in Christ for another time. You might say, "Oh well, I'll repent on my deathbed." But you may not have that opportunity because tomorrow very well might be too late.

Friends, if you are unsaved when you die, that is it. No second chance. God will not hit a replay button on your life. There is no possible way to repent and enter heaven. God says that the time to repent is right now. Immediately open your heart and give your life to Christ Jesus today!

Looking back on this, I came to realize that my life was more important to me than anything. I often think about the air I breathe and what would happen if that was not granted anymore.

As I waited for my surgeries that day, I thought about all that God had revealed to me. Then, I tried calling my mother. I needed to tell her what was happening, but more than that, I needed her to know I loved her. When she didn't answer her phone, I felt a ping of sadness for not being able to reach her; however, little did I know that she was already at a midnight prayer service. She was praying, not knowing what news she would receive later. I called another person, dear to me, my prayer partner. I told her that I was in the hospital, and they were going to perform surgery.

I did not know how it was going to turn out, but I surrendered everything to God. She reassured me that she was going to pray and let other friends and family know so they could also pray for me. Even though they could not physically be with me, I could feel my community surrounding me with their love, and I could feel them going to God on their knees on my behalf.

CHAPTER 19

*Frozen*

Even though the surgeries I had to go through that day were extremely critical, and the doctors thought I would die, we challenged the medical team by putting all our trust in God's provision. My family, friends, prayer partners, and churches who knew about the situation went to the Lord in prayer and fasting, and many of them joined us during that intercessory time. God, our loving and mighty Father, heard our prayers, and the surgeries were successful. My little baby Isaiah was barely three pounds, and he fought for his life the entire time. Luckily, the shot that I had been given (filled with blood thinners) did not damage his brain. We did learn that he had a hole in his heart; however, and that was due to how premature he was.

The doctors informed my husband that with time the hole may close, but it was not guaranteed. In some cases, premature babies that are born with holes in their hearts require open-heart surgery. Isaiah was kept in the hospital in an incubator in the Neonatal Intensive Care Unit (NICU) for nearly two months. He fought for his life with every ounce of his being. Isaiah was destined to be in this world because he fought to gain the weight he needed to survive. As he continued to develop, his weight increased.

I, on the other hand, went into a coma. I never knew what was destined for my baby boy while I was in a coma fighting for my life. I was in the ICU for two months, connected to a ventilator. That machine was the only thing that kept me alive. The doctors told my family that since I had difficulties breathing on my own, I could not stay on the ventilator any longer. They needed to unplug the machine. If I was still unable to breathe on my own after they unplugged it, they would have to perform a tracheotomy. My family disagreed with the idea of surgery because they knew it was a possibility that I could be paralyzed from it.

Instead, my family decided to join their faith in prayer. Shortly after the staff unplugged the ventilator, I was able to breathe on my own. Friends and family— including the hospital staff— were amazed to see what had happened. During the next two months, my family and my community prayed for Isaiah and me constantly. As we both improved little by little, our lives became a living testimony of how God answers prayers.

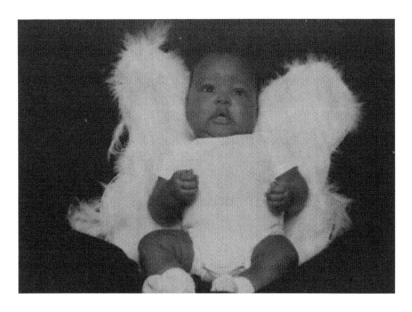

*Isaiah, a few months old*

# CHAPTER 20

## *And God Said, "Let There Be Light"*

It was two months later when I finally woke up. Waking up from that coma was unlike anything I've ever experienced. It was like the sensation of waking up after you had just had a dream of waking up. Everything was fuzzy, and it was difficult to wrap my mind around what was happening. Everything looked strange to me, and even my body felt strange. I remember one of the first things I thought of when I woke up was that I had been pregnant. I remember looking down at my stomach and instantly panicking. I didn't look pregnant anymore. It was only that my mind registered that my mother was in the hospital room with me, and being pregnant was the last thing I remembered. I struggled to rasp out the question that was tearing through my mind, gaining speed like a hurricane.

145

"What happened to my baby?" I finally asked. My throat felt rough like sandpaper from weeks of not being used, and my voice was barely above a whisper. I knew I needed to drink water, but I couldn't rest until I knew what had happened to Isaiah.

"He's fine, Carline. He's in the NICU. He fought bravely, and he's so beautiful."

Her words weren't good enough for me, and I didn't believe her. Memories of what happened began rushing back to me. The flashes of memory were quick and unorganized. I couldn't make sense of what happened, but I did remember the doctors saying that they needed to try and save me instead of the baby because he wasn't going to make it. I began shaking from the stress of it all and the trauma to my body.

"Where is he? Where is my son?"

I demanded to see my baby. I demanded to be told the truth. Each time she insisted that my youngest son was fine, I felt a wave of betrayal. I didn't understand why she was lying to me.

*How could he be fine when I am no longer pregnant and he is nowhere to be seen?*

Finally, my mother showed me a picture of her feeding him in the NICU. When I saw the picture, my heart ached. I wanted to believe it was real, but everything had a dream-like quality. I felt suspended in water from being in a coma for so long. Time had no meaning for me, and simple things were difficult for me to understand. How could my mother be holding and feeding my baby when I hadn't been able to? I had to be sure he was still alive and that she wasn't just trying to protect me.

I asked her to bring him to me so I could hold him. My heart melted from relief when my husband brought both of my sons to visit me the next day. I cried with joy and relief as I held them both in my arms. They were real, and they were both alive. Isaiah left the hospital long before I did, and I longed for the day when I could join my boys and hold my new son.

As I waited in the hospital to recover and go home, my husband walked in one day and told me that there was something he had to tell me right away.

"I have a confession to make." Gerald told me. "Two things, actually. I know you're going to be upset."

"You did name him Isaiah, right?"

While I was still pregnant with our second son, I was reading the book of Isaiah. I already knew that was going to be his name. I was visiting a church one Sunday and in the middle of his sermon, the pastor called me up to the pulpit. I walked up to the pulpit, wondering what the pastor was going to say. I'd never gone to the church before, and the pastor didn't even know who I was. It was a huge mega church in Atlanta, and the walk to the pulpit was a long one.

"You are a special woman…God really loves you." he said.

He prophesied about what my son would become. He didn't know I was going to go into a coma, but he said things about my child that he couldn't possibly have known. Yet again, God was promising good things for me.

Remembering all this, I got very worried that perhaps he didn't name our son Isaiah after all, and I grew fearful. My husband shook his head.

"No, no…but I did use Gerald as a middle name. I signed the birth certificate as Isaiah Gerald Pierre. I would have asked you, but…you know…you were in a coma so I just signed it."

"As long as it's not his first name," I said slowly, thinking about it. "I can deal with that."

"Good," he said. "Good. And, about the other thing…"

I was fairly certain of what he was going to say before he said it.

"After the birth, they performed a hysterectomy." he finally told me.

Had I not been in a coma, I would not have agreed to a hysterectomy. My husband said the doctors told him it was urgent, that they were afraid that I might bleed to death. I imagined that might be part of it, but I was well aware of how his mother felt about me…and how she felt about me having more children. I wanted more children, but she had "advised" me on several occasions. She told me that I needed to stop having kids. I suspected that the real reason was Gerald's mother had talked to him about it, and in turn, Gerald had talked to the doctors. Thanks to my ex-husband, my womb was taken from me.

After I woke up from my coma, it was another month before the hospital would discharge me to go back home. Although I was happy to be back with my family again, my mind still struggled to hold onto reality after spending so much time in the dark. I would find myself saying things to my family that didn't make any sense. I could tell just by the way they looked at me in both a patronizing and scared way that they thought I was losing my mind. Truthfully, even I wondered if I had lost part of myself in that strange plane between life and death. Slowly, I began to regain, sort, and make sense of my memories from when I was in a coma.

# CHAPTER 21

## *Heavenly Visions and Going Home*

Within a matter of days after waking up, I was able to recover many of the memories I had when I was in the coma. I saw fantastic visions that felt less like a dream and more like an alternate reality. They were long, and I remember meeting people I've never seen or heard of. My visions would shift on and off, alternating between periods of enlightenment and darkness. The worst was when I had nightmares. There was no one to wake me up from them, and they felt real. The terror was so vivid that I felt like my psyche would scream in fear. In those visions, I was often being chased by people who tried to harm me, then I would see myself lying on a hospital bed in a huge white room. My mother would always come to my rescue on every dream I had. I suppose that on some level, my subconscious craved the nurturing presence of my mother and recognized that she would often come visit me. It was her presence in those visions that would help calm and soothe me.

In other visions, I would see a place that looked like nothing on Earth. I was flying, soaring through the sky, but I did not know where I was going. It was aimless wandering until I saw two angels dressed in long white robes. As I looked at them, I realized that they had wings and were flying as well. They spoke in a language that I could not understand until one of the angels placed his finger on my lips. Only then, I was able to speak and understand their language.

Suddenly, in the fraction of a moment it takes to blink, we were walking in a beautiful garden. I felt at peace. I felt like I belonged there. Next, the angels took me to another area, where I saw a lot of construction happening. They were building houses of varying sizes down many different streets. I'm not sure how long I watched the development in my visions. At one point, one of the angels left and came back with a delicate crystal plate that had white flatbread. He instructed me to eat it. When I did, he told me that my mission was grand and I needed to go back. I told him that I didn't want to leave. It felt good there, safe, and away from the stress of the world. My mother came to me then and told me I had to go with her. She reached out her hand, and as I took it, I looked back to see the angels only to realize they were gone, and so was the place I can only assume was heaven.

In another dream, I was trapped in a room filled with many different types of people. There were people from all different stages of life as well as healthy and sick people. The room felt like a waiting room of a doctor's office. I heard a loud voice calling each person by their first and last name. At the sound of their name being called, the person would exit through a door and then never return. In my vision, it took an entire day to call everyone through the door. Finally, I was the only person left in the room.

Suddenly, I realized that someone else was in the room with me. I quickly approached him, and I said, "Sir, no one called my name." There was a large part of me that wanted to go where the others went, and I tried to follow them.

The man looked at me, and he smiled before he said, "It's because your time is not up yet. Those people that were called will never come back to this life again. Come with me."

He approached a door that automatically unlocked and opened. He held his arm out, gesturing out of the door and said, "Run for your life." Without needing any further prompting, I raced through the door and didn't look back. In my vision, it took me hours before I finally made it outside.

Then I saw my mother. She told me that she was waiting for me because she knew I needed her.

Looking back, many of the visions I experienced during my coma felt like deja vu. To this day, I wonder if God gave me those visions to better understand the precious mission He has for me. Regardless of the reason for my visions, I know that during my time in the hospital, both conscious and unconscious, I fought for life and, by the grace of God, made it out alive, well, and blessed. My recovery was quick, and I promised myself that just because something traumatic happened to me, I wasn't going to stop living. I had to keep going. After I came out of the hospital, I continued to make tremendous improvements. I worked diligently in my rehabilitation not only to rebuild my physical strength, but also my emotional strength. It took two years for my brain to come to terms with what happened to my body and my soul.

# CHAPTER 22

## *Storm Clouds on the Horizon*

After Isaiah was born, we moved back to Miami with the boys. I was still trying to make things work in my marriage while being a good mother to my boys. I wanted to set a good example for them, and hold myself to the same standard that I would hold them to when they were older. I decided I was going to go back to school. It was a busy time for me, but I was done making excuses. My parents had instilled a love of learning in me, and I knew that my education wasn't something I should put off any longer. I wanted to get my degree.

After high school, I'd taken a couple of college classes and started working on my bachelor's degree. But my health took its toll, and I had to drop out. It was too much for me, to try and balance doctor's visits, my health, and going to school. I'd only been out for a couple of years, but I knew that going to a campus would still be too much for me. I started going to school online, and it was rough. It was just as hard as I thought it'd be— and maybe even harder— to have two little boys, a husband, cook and clean, take care of my health, *and* go to school. But by the grace of God, I got through it.

I was still having difficulty in my marriage, and it escalated to pushing and shoving. It started the night he took my keys so I couldn't leave the house. It was a Friday night, and the church that I attended was having a revival night. Since I was a believer, and he professed to be a believer, I assumed he would have no problem with me going. When I mentioned going to the service together, he made it clear he had no interest in attending. He complained every time I brought it up, even though he knew I had my heart set on going. I needed to be refreshed by the presence of the Lord, but he didn't care. All he cared about was how inconvenient it was to his own plans for me to go to church that night.

I had made up my mind to go without him. I knew he wouldn't be happy about it, and truthfully, he'd told me just what he thought about my willingness to go to church without him several times.

"What would people think if you went without me? Don't you think it will look bad if a woman is in church without her husband?"

He tried to guilt me into staying by claiming that I would not only make myself look bad, but I would also make him look bad in the process. He called me selfish and uncaring, but through it all, I held firm to my desire to go to church.

When I went to leave that Friday night, he started arguing with me again. As he berated me with harsh words, I searched for my keys, desperate to get away from him and run to God. Finally, after I couldn't find them anywhere, I asked him if he had seen my keys. It was then that he sneered at me, mocking me in a way that I didn't think he was capable of…even after I had grown accustomed to all the usual nasty things he'd say about me. He told me that he had my keys and that he wouldn't let me go. My heart felt like it was going to sink in my chest. I was discouraged, just like he wanted, but I wasn't broken. This wasn't the first time he'd tried to keep me from church, and I wasn't going to give up without a fight.

It took hours to convince him to give me my car keys. When I checked the clock, I realized that there was still thirty minutes before church would be over. Catching only the last half hour wasn't what I'd wanted when I set out to go to the revival that night, but at least it was something.

I flew into the building, and before I could sit down, the guest pastor who was preaching stopped and called out to me.

"You there." he said.

I stopped. This man didn't know who I was. Why was he calling out to me? I pointed to myself, and he nodded.

"God told me to tell you that He is going to use you in a very powerful way." he said. "Through you, many lives will be changed and saved. He said you are very anointed, and I see you traveling the world to preach the Gospel."

I sat down, speechless. I knew deep down my heart that God had an appointment with me that day at the service. I had an encounter with God that night. I carried this experience with me back home and harbored it in my heart each time I was pushed or shoved.

I spent time praying on my knees, praying for the Lord to help me understand what He wanted me to do in my marriage. I felt trapped, but I knew that God uses even the most broken people to accomplish wonderful things for His glory. I would often think of the prostitute, Rahab, and how God used her to carry out the line of David, the very line that Jesus was born into. Rahab's life was filled with brokenness, but God still used her to glorify His name. I wasn't sure how God would use me, but I had faith that somehow He would work out my abusive situation for His good.

As both the physical and verbal abuse got worse, Gerald's rage was followed by apologies, then he would harass me to 'makeup' and have sex with him. He would say things like; 'if you loved me, you would,' or 'I just love you so much' and 'you make me so angry, if you would just do what I say we wouldn't have these problems.' These phrases echoed through my mind at all hours of the day and during the long hours of the night. They hammered me down and shackled me in chains. They made me feel small and helpless, but the worst part of all was that they taunted me with a love I could only have if I was good enough to deserve it.

The way I saw my husband changed.

The situation was still the same; we fought and he physically abused me. One time I called the cops, and they came and questioned both me and my sons. I'd lied to them, just like I'd lied to them the first time I ever called the cops, but my children exposed me. I told the cops that they had been safely locked away in their room while the fight was happening. They were questioned again at school, and after the officers asked my sons about what had happened, they told them that, "daddy was choking mommy."

But the real last straw was when he started yelling at my mother. He and I were fighting, and while I was used to the horrible things he would say to me, I wasn't expecting him to disrespect my mother like that. He started yelling at her, and suddenly, I saw him for who he really was. No one talks to my family like that. Not only that, but I realized how toxic my husband was, and I didn't want my sons to grow up with that kind of example. I'd protected my husband for years, but now it was time for me to protect both myself and my boys.

I told Gerald he needed to leave. I told him he had to go, and that the boys would be staying with me. He left, and moved back to North Carolina to be with his family. I still didn't tell my parents much about what happened. Eventually, they knew, but it was over now, and I didn't want my father or brothers to beat him up. I just wanted it to be over and done with. I wanted a fresh start for me and my boys. I didn't want to be reminded of all the things my ex-husband had put me through. I stayed with my parents, and reconnected with my family. It felt good to finally be home and be around people who loved me.

I found out later that Gerald had also been cheating on me (multiple times, in fact). We'd separated once or twice temporarily, and when we did, he'd been involved with a married woman. While we were still married, I'd been sent a *Facebook* message by the husband of one of the women that Gerald had been having an affair with. I didn't see it until years later. Because *Facebook* hides message requests from people you're not friends with, I had no idea it was even sent until two or three years later. The message confirmed a few suspicions I had, but I no longer cared at that point. I saw it as yet another confirmation that leaving Gerald was the right thing to do.

I tried filing for divorce, and it ended up being a horribly long process. I had to go back and forth to the lawyer's office and the courthouse for the endless paperwork associated with divorce. There was always mix-ups, and it was drawn out longer than it should have. When I was finally ready to file, I was told that I didn't need to. I didn't need to because Gerald had already filed. I found out later that the reason he filed for a divorce is because he needed to go to Haiti to marry his new wife.

I leaned heavily on the firm foundation of faith my parents had instilled within me. I pressed into the example I saw growing up and prayed that God would provide for our needs. He did so, abundantly. It was a blessing to watch the Lord continue to provide for me as I carved out a new life for myself and my boys. I knew that life wouldn't be perfect from here on out, but I was strengthened by how God had never left me or forsaken me. Two Bible verses that have always stuck in my mind for how God's presence has never deserted me are from the book of Jeremiah.

"Before I formed you in the womb I knew you, before you were born I set you apart." (Jeremiah 1:5)

"'For I know the plans I have for you,' declares the Lord, 'plans to prosper you and not to harm you, plans to give you hope and a future.'" (Jeremiah 29:11)

One day a very good friend of mine, Bishop Marc—whom I look up to as a spiritual mentor said to me, "Carline, you're going to get through this. You will love again, laugh again and dream again. The right man is going to come along, and he's going to love you the right way and you're going to forget all your past hurt."

That was the last thing I wanted to hear. Hearing the word 'love' in that moment was like pouring vinegar on my wound. I was bitter. I said, "Bishop, I have high expectations and I refuse to settle for less than what God has for me."

"You won't settle," he said. "God will give you what you deserve because He has the best for you."

Soon after our conversation I started thinking about my future, my purpose, and my children. I convinced myself that I had to forgive my ex-husband, but I didn't know how I was going to do that because I was wounded. In order to move forward, I needed to forgive him. The road to forgiveness was a journey itself, but I was excited that I was making steps toward healing.

Each time I studied, meditated and prayed, I was reminded that God has always had my best interest at heart and that He would always turn even my darkest circumstances into a beacon of light. I was ready to hope for a brighter future.

I stayed in Miami for the next three years. I loved living close to family, and my boys were having fun getting reacquainted with everyone. My parents helped watch the boys while I went to work, and the three of us were healing and starting over from the life we had led.

I began working hard to provide for my family now that I was the breadwinner. I started my own skincare and shampoo company and threw all my energy into my work. About a year and a half after I left my husband, I started growing restless. I started feeling smothered. I went from not having any family nearby, to family around me all the time. I love my family a lot, but it was too much togetherness. The boys and I needed more space. I had no intentions of leaving Florida, I never did, but I knew that I needed to start looking for a change of pace. We needed a place where it was just us, and nobody else.

It was around this time I started talking to my friend Beatrice on a regular basis. A few years back, Beatrice had announced she was getting married. I was thrilled for her, and when she asked me to be her maid of honor, I was even more thrilled. I like to go all out for people, and I thought it would be a nice surprise for me to pay for Beatrice's entire reception. I wanted to help take some of the burden off of her, and I was more than happy to do it. But after examining my savings account, I was devastated when I realized there was no way I could afford *everything* I wanted to do for Beatrice. I had such grand plans for what I wanted to do for her, and it crushed me when I realized I couldn't give her everything I thought she deserved.

With a heavy heart, I told Beatrice that I thought someone else would be better. She seemed confused, but I eventually convinced her she should find someone who would be able to dedicate more time and attention to the wedding planning and all the little small details that came with it. I told her that it was too much for me to take on. That was partially true, but it wasn't the only reason.

I ended up not even going to the wedding or the reception. I did go over to the church and I did everyone's hair and makeup. I did the whole wedding party...hair, makeup...everything, and it became my wedding gift to Beatrice. After I finished, I packed up my tools, and I went home. And that was that.

Beatrice and I reconnected. She attended the same church I did, and the boys loved her. She loved them, too, and would play with them. That's how we got so close. She became like an auntie to my boys, and because my boys loved her, I loved her, too.

She told me that she had moved to Texas, and that anytime I wanted to, I should move out there with her. They had an extra room in the apartment, and they'd help me with the boys.

"Come on!" she'd say. "Move to Texas, we'll open up a salon together and we'll run it together and work together, it'll be fun!"

I'd turned her offer down a couple of times, and each time, she'd reassure me that the offer would still stand no matter what. I'd laugh it off, and we'd hang up. It seemed like a bad idea for the first couple of years she brought it up, but when I started growing restless from the lack of space in Miami, I figured it couldn't hurt, and seriously considered her offer. I called her up, asked her if she was still open to starting a business together. She told me to pack up and get myself on a plane.

So we did. I left my car in Florida until I could figure out a way to get it cross country. I wanted to take it with me, but it was too far to drive by myself with the boys. We loaded what we could carry into our suitcases, and Gecarr, Isaiah and I, flew to Texas. Beatrice and her family welcomed me with open arms, and it felt like the move was a step in the right direction.

Because I wasn't able to be her maid of honor, Beatrice told me I could be the godmother to her son, Derrick. I was incredibly excited, and bought him toys and gifts and spoiled him as often as I could. Not too long after, I'd spoken to a mutual friend, and she said that she was out buying things for Derrick because she was his godmother.

"What?" I said. "You're kidding, right?"

"No. Why?" she asked.

"Because *I'm* Derrick's godmother." I told her.

"But…" she started. "*I'm* Derrick's godmother."

Neither one of us said anything for a while, and then, even though she was clearly upset, she broke out laughing.

"Well," she said. "I guess there's two of us!"

We both learned later that Beatrice had appointed at least three of her other friends to be Derrick's godmother as well. Unlucky for us, but lucky Derrick had five godmothers. It was the small things like this that should have clued me into the kinds of stuff that Beatrice did, but at the time, it just stung.

The boys and I moved into the extra bedroom. We'd all help raise and watch the kids when we weren't working, but I spent most of my free time searching for a job. Beatrice's husband worked at a fast food restaurant not too far away from their apartment. He was friends with the manager and told me he could get me a job right away.

"Yeah, that's no problem, listen, honestly…you could start tomorrow." he told me, excitedly. "I'll do that for you. I have the hook up. You just say the word and the job is yours."

He was so excited at the thought of getting me the job, and I could not have been less excited. I'd worked in banking or the financial industry my entire adult life…what would I accomplish by working at a fast food joint? I have nothing against hard work, and I wouldn't dream of mocking anyone on account of what they do for a living, but I was not about to work in fast food. I had my degree, I worked in banking…I was going to get a job in banking.

"No, thank you." I told him. "I'll find something else soon enough."

And so I began job hunting. I looked for everything and anything that might be a fit for me. I searched for jobs in the financial industry and banking and anything close to banking. True, I wanted to start my own business, but I needed a steady stream of income first. I could work on my business in the off hours when I wasn't already on the clock somewhere else.

I found a job that seemed almost too good to be true. I applied and waited to hear back for an interview (which I got). I still hadn't had time to bring my car up from Florida, so I borrowed their car to go to the interview. I got the job, and even though it was a little farther than I would have liked, it was a good job. I was excited to start.

"I got the job!" I announced, as I walked in the house.

"Oh, hun, that's great!" Beatrice said. "When do you start?"

"A week from Tuesday." I said, handing her back her keys.

Just then her husband walked into the room, and I told him the good news. He smiled and nodded, and asked me where it was and how far it was from the house. I told him, and his smile vanished.

"That's so far." he said. "Why would you want to go so far? Just work somewhere near here."

He shook his head again and again, and I wondered if I was missing something. It wasn't *that* far, it really wasn't, and I was more than willing to make it work.

"Umm, that's really too far…that's too many miles… to put on the car…" his voice trailed off.

Still not sure why it was a problem, I took a moment to collect my thoughts. Finally I said, "Then I'll take the bus. I'll do whatever I have to do. Really, it's not that far."

He shrugged, acting like he'd tried his best to dissuade me, then walked out of the room, and that was the end of the conversation.

I got the job and I worked and worked and worked. I was saving all my money while I watched my credit score go up. Since I wasn't paying rent, I supplied the house with groceries. Every two weeks, I'd go to the store and spend at least three hundred dollars on food and toiletries. I figured it was my contribution to keep the house running smoothly. I was spending six hundred a month, easy, and I was happy to do it.

And it wasn't just food. If I was out shopping for Gecarr or Isaiah for clothes or school supplies, I'd pick up something for her boys, too. I didn't think it was right to buy my children something if her children weren't going to get anything, so I always picked something up for them as well.

Beatrice's brother-in-law and her sister, Caroline, lived nearby. Every Saturday evening, they'd swing by with their two daughters and me and my sons would pray with them. I needed the fellowship, and we'd pray together and encourage one another. They were lovely, caring people, so I was surprised when Beatrice and her husband told me to stay away from them.

"Why?" I asked.

"Because," Beatrice said. "Because, they're just…"

She shook her head, and her husband finished the sentence for her.

"They're just not good people. We don't want you hanging out with them."

I found it all weird and suspicious, and it did make me wonder if they were hiding something. I told them I was an adult, and I'd do as I pleased, and I left it at that.

We'd been living together for a couple of months in the apartment. My job paid me extremely well, so even with all the money I'd been spending on food and groceries, I still had plenty to put away every month. I started looking for our own place. We'd always lived with someone, and it was time to move out on our own. I wanted the boys to have their own room, and I wanted a home where I could call the shots. It would be *our* home and no one else's.

I don't remember how it came up, but somehow, they found out how much money I was making, and their whole attitude toward me changed. They went from being the warm and friendly people I'd always known, to cold, distant, and negative roommates. They started acting sneaky, and I later found out from my boys that while I was at work, they made them watch their kids. So while my sons were supposed to be doing their homework, they were really babysitting her kids.

The husband came to me one day and told me that he wanted rent money. Knowing that they only paid eight hundred dollars a month in rent and that I was paying close to that just for groceries, I found the request a little ridiculous. While I hadn't told them yet, I'd already found a place, and would be moving there in less than three weeks.

"This isn't how I wanted to tell you," I said. "But I actually already found a place…so I can't pay rent because I'm actually already going to be moving out with my boys."

"You're moving out?" he said. "You're moving out and you didn't tell me?"

"That's why I'm telling you right now."

"So you're not going to be paying me any rent? You're not paying me any rent at all?"

"No. Because I'm moving out."

He stared at me for a moment, and then he walked away. I figured that was the end of it. But the next morning, however, I was woken up by the sound of boxes and moving furniture. I left my room to see what was going on.

"Pass me that, will you?" Beatrice asked her husband.

"What is going on in here?" I asked.

They didn't stop moving for a minute.

"We're moving." he said.

I was speechless.

"I'm sorry, you're what? You're moving?"

"That's right." he said, taping a box up. "We're moving out today."

"You're moving out *today*?" I repeated, completely bewildered.

"Yes." he nodded. "I'm telling you, we're moving out today. You're going to have to pay the rent."

I watched them pack up everything they owned. I wasn't really sure what else to do, so I went back into my room. A few hours later, Caroline and her husband stopped by (as they did every Saturday) and saw the commotion. They pulled me aside and talked to me in hushed tones.

"I walked out this morning and they're packing." I told them. "They're packing up everything and they're moving."

"They do that. They used to live with us and they did the same thing."

"Just like that?"

"Just like that." he said. "Do you have a place to go?"

I shook my head.

"My place isn't going to be ready for another three weeks."

"Listen, Carline, I'll tell you what you're going to do…"

"Okay," I said, and waited for him to continue.

"I have a big house, a really big house. We have like five bedrooms. We're not using all the space. We'll come over and help you get your stuff, and you and the boys will move in with us until your place is ready."

And that's what we did. I'm so grateful that I didn't listen to what Beatrice and her husband had said; Caroline's family was there for me when I needed them. God is faithful, and we had a place to go. We lived with them for the next three weeks, just like they said, and then we got the keys to our new apartment, and they helped us move in. They later told me that Beatrice and her husband stayed in their apartment for another nine months before they actually moved out.

As we thanked them and waved goodbye, I suddenly remembered something I had said the year before. Last Christmas, I was living with my parents and I had told God that I wanted to be settled in a new place by the next Christmas. You have to be careful what you tell God, because He listens.

We got a tree, and in our empty new place, we danced around the Christmas tree, thanking God for everything we had. The apartment may have been empty, but it was everything we needed. Not only was it ours, but it was even bigger and better than the last apartment. It was our home for the next two years.

On the third year, I decided not to renew the lease. I started house hunting. My realtor found us a gorgeous, beautiful five bed, four bath, three car garage. The paperwork was nearly done, the inspection completed, and we were only waiting on a few small technicalities before we could officially move in. Everything in my life was so effortless and smooth, and I couldn't wait to see what else the future held for me.

Between work and my commute, I was really busy in Texas, but because of that, we started developing our own unique family traditions. For the first time in our lives, we were free to become a family.

We bonded a lot during the Texas years, and we learned a lot about each other. For example, my boys are very friendly. They'll stop and chat with people in the mall about the weather or their favorite sports teams or just to comment on how much they liked that person's shirt. No part of me is that friendly. I love people, but I have no desire to strike up a random conversation with someone standing in the line in front of me.

*Starting over in Texas*

We developed a healthy line of open communication. As much as I loved my parents and did incorporate their parenting style into my own, I started doing things differently. When I was growing up, my parents and I had open communication. They still knew everything about my life, and they still talked to me about all the same things I talk about with my sons. The difference is that me and my siblings would get in trouble. We knew that we could tell our parents anything, but we also knew we'd be in a lot of trouble.

I didn't want my kids to be scared to tell me things. I didn't want them to hide something from me out of fear of getting punished. I didn't want that for my sons, so I decided to change things. I established an open door policy, and we talked about everything from the importance of school, religion, their thoughts on life, and why they wouldn't be dating anyone until they were out of college.

I guess that part stayed the same.

We still ate very healthy because of my Cardiac diet, and because I wanted them to have a healthy outlook on food and nutrients. I would cook at home every weeknight except for Friday. Friday was always pizza night, and we looked forward to it every week. We'd hang out the rest of the weekend and go out to eat, go to the movies on Saturday, do laundry, grocery shop, and go to church services on Sunday and spend time with our church friends.

On birthdays and special occasions we'd go out for seafood and sushi. The birthday person would get their own small personal birthday cake that they didn't have to share. It made it special, fun, and just a little bit healthier.

I have smart children, and I'm very proud of them, and always will be. I'm proud of the open communication we have and that my children know that they can come to me with anything. I've only not been completely honest with them once.

When Gecarr was about five years old and Isaiah was four, they started wondering how old I was. They were so very curious about everything, including how old their parents were. First they went to Gerald and asked him how old he was. After they had that bit of information they came over and asked me the same thing.

"I can't tell you my age," I told them.

"Why not, mummy?"

"Because," I said. "it's a secret."

Their eyes got big and they stared up at me in wonder.

"A secret?"

I held on for a while before giving them a number. When I finally did tell them how old I was…well, let's just say I turned eighteen for a couple of birthdays.

"But you must promise not to tell anyone. You must promise me that you won't tell anyone my age. Promise?"

They nodded and swore themselves to secrecy. Knowing how friendly they were, I wasn't sure how long it would last. At my next birthday, they started adding years to my age, but I continued to remind them that mummy only turned eighteen. That was as old as mummy got.

I picked them up from school one day, and Isaiah told me all about his teacher and his friends and how old his friend's parents were.

"And Jamarian says you are old enough to vote, mummy."

I glanced in the rearview mirror and caught sight of Isaiah's smiling face.

"Oh?" I asked. "And how does Jamarian know how old I am?"

The smile immediately faded from his face. He looked over at Gecarr, who was wearing the same look of pure terror.

"Oopsie, mummy. I didn't mean to. I'm sorry."

And with that, the grins returned, and I continued being eighteen for a few more years. It wasn't until I asked Gecarr to get my license for me a few years later that he finally saw my birth year. He walked up to me, grinning from ear to ear. He handed me my wallet.

"I know how old you are." he said.

"What are you talking about? No, you don't."

He nodded, then looked at the wallet.

"I saw. I know how old you are!"

I managed to hide my age for ten years before they learned how old I really was.

After Gerald and I separated, there was minimal contact. While in Texas, he wanted to know where we lived, and my father refused to tell him. He acted as a buffer between us. Even if Gerald said he wanted to 'send the boys presents' and that's why he needed our address, my father still told him no.

"If you have something for the boys, send it to my house. I'll make sure Carline gets them."

He never once sent presents, it was just his way of trying to figure out where we were. I called him maybe once or twice in regards to the boys, but after this conversation, I never called him again:

"Hi, Gerald."

"Hi, Carline. What do you want?"

"It's about the boys."

Silence.

"Look," I said. "They're your boys, too. And I've been taking care of them and providing for them since you left…"

"So?" he retorted.

"So I think you should send some money for the boys…I have the apartment and the car and everything… you're their father. You should send money for clothes and school supplies if the boys need them."

"The boys need clothes?" he asked.

"Yes."

"Then you should get off your a** and get a job." he growled. "*You* get the boys clothes."

"Okay." I said. "No problem."

I hung up the phone and resolved never to ask him for anything again. I didn't want to force him into child support. I would bring it up sometimes, after he'd say that he was the boy's father and that he needed to see them, or whenever he wanted something from me.

"You still haven't sent any money." I'd say.

"I'll send it tomorrow, I'll send it tomorrow. It'll get there, no problem. I promise." he'd say, even though he still never sent anything.

Carline in South Africa

I learned to ignore his empty promises and his calls came less and less often.

My life clouded over in April of 2019.

In March, I'd flown to South Africa for a mission trip. Not wanting to leave the boys alone, I had thought about flying them to Florida to stay with my parents for a while. The idea was short-lived when I saw how much it would be for a round trip ticket for both. They were still minors, and the cost of hiring an accompanying adult was more than I wanted to pay. I decided I'd fly my dad to Texas, and he could stay with my sons until I came back. Everything went according to plan. I flew my dad to our apartment, went to Africa, came back, and sent my dad home. It was less than a week later when all my troubles started.

I was headed to work when I suddenly felt a sharp stabbing pain in my chest right below my breast bone. I was preoccupied with getting to work on time, so when I felt the pain, I assumed it would go away in a few minutes or, at worst, a few hours. I had no reason to think that it was any indication of a serious health problem. I had been healthy for some time and continued to eat a balanced Cardiac diet, exercised, and minimized my stress as much as possible.

But the pain didn't stop. In fact, it increased. By noon, I was in so much pain that I asked my manager if he had some *Tylenol* I could take. At that point, I was desperate for relief, and when the *Tylenol* did nothing for me, I decided that it was best to go to the emergency room. My stomach knotted in anxiety as I tried to decide if I should go to the closest emergency room, or if it would be better to travel to the one closer to my home, which was thirty minutes away from my job.

When my manager advised me to go to the ER closest to my home, I immediately jumped in my car. I prayed the entire drive there and tried not to concentrate on the growing intensity of my pain. When I arrived at the hospital, I wasn't sure what they would say my diagnosis was. The type of pain I was having was unlike anything else I had experienced before. I wasn't sure if it was a problem with my heart, or something else. However, after running several diagnostic exams, they informed me an hour later that I had gallstones, a hardened section of digestive fluid that formed in my gallbladder. I was stunned as they explained that I would need to be transported to another hospital in order to have a surgery that would remove my gallbladder.

After the surgery, I was discharged home the next day with hopes of an easy, uncomplicated recovery. However, two days after my operation, I started feeling an intense pain that was even worse than the pain I felt from my gallstones. My stomach and my legs quickly began to swell. I remember pressing them lightly with my fingertips and feeling like my body was inflamed. My skin was taut from the swelling and I felt like I was a bike tire that was being pumped up with too much air. I knew immediately that something was very wrong. I returned to the hospital. I wasn't prepared for what they told me.

## CHAPTER 23

*Hurricanes without Rainbows*

I was experiencing heart failure.

As soon as they discovered I was experiencing heart failure again, they admitted me to the hospital. I stayed there for three weeks receiving IV fluids and antibodies. The doctors hoped that it would bring me out of heart failure, but the fluid traveled down to my lungs and I developed Pulmonary hypertension. Most people in my situation would have been crushed by the development, but for me, it was a strange relief. I had been struggling to breathe for a while, and my diagnosis meant that there was a medical plan for solving it. My relief was short-lived, however, when they informed me that the only way they could resolve my issue was to have me undergo another open heart surgery as well as undergo immediate lung surgery. It was unfortunate news that resulted in a lot of waiting around.

Because I was stuck in the hospital for almost a month, my parents rotated watching the boys. If they were busy or if they were in the hospital with me, I'd get a family friend or church member to sit with Gecarr and Isaiah for a few hours after they got home from school. Gecarr was fourteen at the time and Isaiah was thirteen, but they were still too young to be left alone that long. I worried about them constantly. If I knew someone was there to make sure they were fed and that they had gotten home okay, I worried a little less.

One day, a church member was going to check on them until my parents got home from the hospital. She was bringing food for dinner and was going to stay with the boys for a couple of hours. She wouldn't be there before they got home from school, but they wouldn't be alone for too long before she got there. I didn't give her a key because Gecarr knew who was coming on which day and what time they'd be there, so he would unlock the door and let them in until one of the family members got back.

It must have been around four in the afternoon when she got there, about an hour after school let out. She parked her car, grabbed the food, and knocked on the door. She waited for a while, and then knocked louder, but there was still no sign of the boys. She knocked a final third time, and then gave up. She dialed my cell phone, and I could tell she was trying not to alarm me.

"Hey, Carline."

"Hey. Are you at the house?"

"Yes. Um…what time did their school let out?"

"About an hour ago."

"Okay. Okay…so they should be here, right?"

"They're not there?!"

I panicked. I could nearly feel my blood pressure rising.

"Well, I don't see them…Maybe they missed the bus?"

"Did you knock?"

"Of course I knocked!" she said. "Don't you think I knocked?"

"Okay, okay." I said. "Let me call them and I'll call you back."

"Okay."

I hung up and dialed the house phone. It rang and rang and rang. No answer. By now I was really scared, and I was genuinely considering checking myself out of the hospital, driving home, and checking on my boys. It didn't matter that it would have been a physical impossibility for me to do so; I was about thirty seconds away from trying my luck.

"Mom." I said. "Did you hear that?"

"They're not there?"

"I don't understand. Why wouldn't they be there?" I asked, mainly to myself, but my mother answered.

"Don't panic yet." she said. "Call the school."

I dialed again. The secretary answered.

"Hi, this is Carline Edouard."

"Hi, Carline."

"My sons Gecarr and Isaiah were supposed to be home an hour ago, but the sitter's there and she said they're not... there."

"Well, we haven't been told otherwise..."

"You haven't been told otherwise?" I repeated.

"As far as we know they made it on the bus."

I buried my face in my hands. It felt like we were on the verbal merry-go-round and there were no concrete answers anywhere.

"Hold on, Miss Edouard...let me check with a few people and I'll get back to you."

She hung up, and in the meantime, I called the sitter back.

"Still nothing?" I asked.

"Still nothing." she replied. "Did you try the school?"

"Of course I tried the school."

"What did they say?"

"I'm waiting for them to call me back."

"Okay," she said. "You let them call you back and then I'll wait for you to call me back."

As we hung up a second time, my mother looked up from her book.

"I take it they're still not there?"

"No, mom. They're still not there."

I groaned. I was unbelievably stressed out by the whole situation. My mind wandered to all kinds of horrible scenarios. Did they get kidnapped? Did they not make it onto the bus? Had someone else picked them up?

*Someone else couldn't have picked them up...the school doesn't allow anyone beside the legal guardian to pick up the kids unless they have written consent or have been told beforehand. The car line for pick ups is in an entirely different lane...there's no way that could have happened.*

My phone rang.

"Yes, hello Miss Edouard?"

"Yeah, I'm here."

"So, we've talked to a few of the students, and one of Gecarr's classmates said that he thought he saw Gecarr get into a vehicle."

"One of the classmates did?"

"Yes, ma'am. That is correct, but none of the staff can visually confirm that, so—"

"So you really have no idea?"

Silence.

"Again, ma'am, we can't really be held responsible for...."

"But I never gave permission for anyone to pick them up. You can't release them unless I've called before to tell you that someone other than a member of the family was going to be picking them up."

"Well, Gecarr's classmate said that it looked like Gecarr knew him…"

"Let me get this straight…" I began, trying to withhold the rage I felt toward the secretary and the entire school board. "You think, based on what a teenage student said, that it looked like Gecarr got into someone's car…that it looked like he knew the person…but no one in the office actually saw what happened."

"…Yes, Miss Edouard. That is correct."

I was hooked up to machines, tired and exhausted because I could barely sleep due to the pain, and I was getting no straight answers from anyone. I was growing more frustrated and irritated by the minute, and I really was about ready to get out of my bed and track down my sons.

My phone started beeping.

"Hang on." I said. "I'm getting another call."

I hung up.

"Hello?" I said. "Hello?"

"Oh, hi, mummy."

"…Gecarr?"

"Yes." Gecarr's slurred voice came through the other end of the phone. "Sorry we didn't answer the phone. When we got home Isaiah and I were so tired that we just passed out."

"You passed out?"

"Yes…" Gecarr yawned. "Mummy. We passed out. We were so tired."

"And you didn't think to call me, or grandpa, or grandma, or *anybody*?"

"No, we just walked right in the door and passed out."

I didn't know if I should be mad, relived, or amused. I'd gotten so worked up and stressed out over the whole ordeal, that even though I wanted to feel relieved, I was too worked up to fully relax. My sons— who had completely tuned out the knocking at the door and ignored or slept through the phone, whatever you want to call it— had the nerve to tell me that they were tired and fell asleep when they had everyone all worked up and terrified for them.

"Oh," I heard Gecarr say. "Oh, it's that lady at the front door. Should I let her in?"

I tried to take a deep breath (as deep a breath as I could with all the fluid in my lungs) and wait a moment before answering.

"Mummy?" Gecarr asked. "Mummy, should I let her in?"

"Yes, Gecarr. You should definitely let the sitter in."

"Okay." he responded, slowly waking up. "Okay, we will do that."

He barely pulled the phone away from his mouth before he yelled at Isaiah to open the door.

"So how are you, mummy?" Gecarr asked, innocently, and completely oblivious to the fine mess he had created.

I talked to Gecarr for a while longer before eventually hanging up the phone. I was trying to rest when my phone rang the final time; it was the school.

"Yes, hello Miss Edouard?"

"We found them. They're fine. They're at home."

"That's wonderful news, Miss Edouard. I'm so glad that we could—"

I hung up.

I worried for my boys, my family, and my health. Once again, I became cold as ice because I could not comprehend what was happening to me in such a short period of time. The doctors told me that my case was very complicated and I needed to discharge myself and go to another hospital because they were not equipped to perform heart surgery.

I didn't know what to do. I'd had to fly both my parents back out less than a week after my father had gone back to Florida. They didn't want to stay in Texas, and my health was getting increasingly worse. The realtor wanted to close on my house, telling me that we could start the paperwork even though I was going to be in and out of hospitals. She nearly convinced me to do it, but after talking it over with my parents, we decided it would be best to hold off on the house until I at least got a referral to another hospital where they could perform the surgery.

The hospital staff told us that they sent referrals to two different hospitals, but both had denied the request. They used the excuse that they didn't have any rooms available. I heard the excuse, but I had a sinking feeling that the reason they denied me was because they didn't think my surgery would be a success.

It seemed that no one had faith that I would come out of my surgery alive. I had once again been shoved to the side as another statistic. Near the end of my three week stay, one of the charge nurses came into my room. She rapidly tapped her pencil against the clipboard in her hands.

"Look, I'm almost off, and I don't want you dying on my shift, so you need to hurry up and get out of here."

My mother was shocked. I was surprised at how direct she was being.

*Can they even say something like that to a patient? What a horrible thing to say!*

"What is it you expect us to do?" my mother asked her. "Look at her...she's in critical condition. You can't move her."

The nurse shrugged.

"Why don't you call an *Uber* to take you to another hospital?"

"Okay, well, could you put her in an ambulance to take her to the hospital and send her over as an emergency transfer? That way they'd see her faster than if she checks herself into another hospital."

I was shocked when the nurse explained that I needed to go to another hospital on my own.

"They'll see you faster." she claimed, and walked out of the room.

I didn't know if she was right or not. But at that point, I was frantic for some type of medical assistance. I didn't understand how I was supposed to advocate for myself when no one would hear me out. After searching for any nearby hospitals that would take me into their care, my parents finally decided to move me back to Florida because we had no family in Texas and none of the hospitals would take on my case. *None.* It seemed like the best move for me, but when we asked the doctor to give us a referral to fly to Florida, he denied our request. We were told that, due to my hypertension, it was highly likely that the change of air pressure in the plane would make it impossible for me to breathe, and I would die.

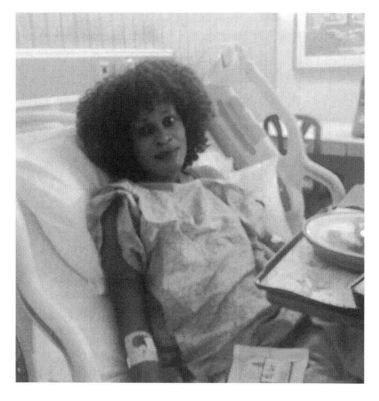

Picture of Carline in the Texas hospital

I tried my best not to cry as I realized the hospital was more concerned about me being just another number to increase their death toll than actually getting me the help I so desperately needed. I was so frustrated with them that I decided the best thing for me to do was to discharge myself; the hospital clearly wasn't going to try and help me at all.

When I went to file the paperwork, the nurse informed me that she had already discharged me hours ago. I couldn't help but think that she had discharged me to die at home. My parents, on the other hand, encouraged me to look at being discharged as a blessing in disguise. My mother reminded me of how God has delivered me through every trial in the past and how He would continue to do it again. It was difficult to see any hope in such a bad situation, but at least I was leaving such a negligent place.

# CHAPTER 24

## *More Waiting*

Together, my parents, my sons, and I got on a two and half hour flight from Texas to Florida. I clutched my chair's armrests the entire flight, waiting for the air to get crushed out of my lungs; waiting for the moment I would stop breathing and die. As we landed safe and sound in Florida, we praised God for His mercy. Against all medical odds, I was alive.

I made my way to the local hospital as quickly as I could. I was once again being rushed off the plane for a life-saving surgery. When I arrived I was greeted by the Cardiac team. They ran several tests on me to determine how quickly my hypertension had escalated. After getting the results back, they were hesitant to perform the heart surgery I would need in order to survive. They were afraid that my lungs were too weakened to withstand any kind of surgery, and they were certain I would die on the table.

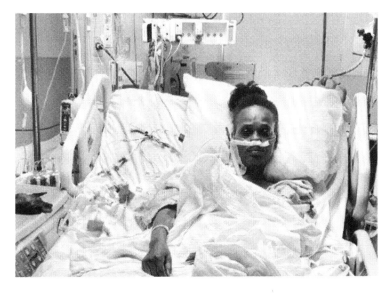

*Carline awaiting her third open heart surgery.*
*Photographed by Sir T. Renesca*

This was followed by lots of waiting around and constantly being told different things from the different surgical teams. There's not a lot to do in the hospital, and you see the staff more than anyone else, so you end up talking to and getting to know the nurses. One of the nurses and I talked about kids, and ex-husbands and child support. I told her that I didn't want to guilt Gerald into paying for child support.

"He doesn't pay child support?!" she exclaimed, glancing up from the IV. "What do you mean, he doesn't pay child support?"

I shrugged

"I didn't want to force him."

"So what do you do for insurance?" she asked.

"We don't have insurance."

The nurse sighed, and patted my hand. I couldn't tell if she wanted to laugh at me or yell at me.

"You know that if you have child support you qualify for insurance, right?"

"What, for medicare?"

She nodded.

"Honey, make that man pay child support. It certainly isn't going to hurt him."

At her prodding, I finally filed for child support. I was unemployed, stuck in the hospital, and desperate to figure out a way to pay for the surgeries I needed. Sure enough, it qualified us for medicare, and it was one less thing for me to worry about.

Since my Pulmonary team and Cardiology team didn't have a coinciding plan of action, I was discharged two weeks after I was admitted. When I went home, I was tempted to fall back into depression. I played back what each of the medical teams had said. The Pulmonary team said after the heart surgery was done then they could start a treatment plan for my lungs. On the other side, the Cardiology team said that before they could operate on my heart, my lungs had to be treated because the pressure was too high to withstand surgery. My head was spinning as I tried to make heads or tails of what the best path for me was moving forward. I struggled with understanding why God would allow me to go through so much difficulty in life. It felt like I was no longer enduring His purification and sanctification process, but that I was under fire from the enemy.

*Here we go again...more heart problems....*

I tried my best to use prayer and supplication as a means to distract myself from the physical pain, but one week after being discharged, I returned. This pattern continued for nearly two months. I would go to the hospital, nearly in tears from how much constant pain I was in, the doctors would give me medication to treat my symptoms, and would send me home. Once I was home, I tried my best to rest and heal, but the pain would attack me like a vicious monster, and I would hurry back to the hospital. Out of nowhere, God sent me another angel, but this time, it was in the form of Dr. Roger Argelio Alvarez.

While Dr. Alvarez was one of the best Pulmonologists in South Florida, I wasn't sure what to expect. The doctors I had in the past always wrote me off as another death statistic.

*What would make Dr. Alvarez any different? Would he see me as a person? Or a puzzle that could be dismissed if it proved to be too challenging?*

I prayed before my visit and asked God to ease my anxiety and discouragement. When I arrived, I was thrilled to discover that Dr. Alvarez was wonderful to work with. He made the process very comfortable and he quickly started me on a treatment plan for my lungs.

He was the first person who advised me that he believed that I would survive the surgeries. I was ecstatic to hear his opinion. He could see that my life meant something, and he was willing to prove to the world that I was more than a statistic. He recognized that my life was on the line, and he tried to treat my lungs for as long as he could before my open-heart surgery. We knew we had to take action when my mitral valve went from leaking to completely tearing. June 28 of 2019, I was admitted to the hospital to have my surgery. Dr. Alvarez referred me to one of the best Cardiac surgeons alive— who happened to be on vacation at the time— and was instrumental in scheduling an appointment for me. I would still have to wait until he returned from vacation to be seen. While I was in the hospital, I prayed everyday that my heart would make it until Dr. Lamelas' return, so that I could have the surgery I once again so desperately needed.

## CHAPTER 25

### *Familiar Battlefield*

When Dr. Lamelas returned, he immediately set a date for my open-heart surgery. Three days before the surgery, I had the scariest experience of my life, and it almost killed me. When it happened, I was still in an immense amount of pain, but I was remaining strong through it because I knew that I would be having surgery in a few days. Suddenly, in addition to the horrific pain, I had shortness of breath, nausea, broke out in a cold sweat, and my blood pressure (which was previously always low) plummeted and my heart rate rhythm changed completely. I didn't lose consciousness, but the machines signaled a code, and a team of nurses and doctors came running into the room. They quickly connected me to an automated external defibrillator ready to shock me when my heart actually stopped. I saw my life flash right in front of my eyes and all I could think about was my boys.

I was dying. I heard the doctors and nurses telling me to, "Breathe, breathe. You can do this…just breathe." Another smaller voice in the distance told me, "Don't give up. Breathe." Even though I could hear everything they were saying, I didn't know how to do it. Breathing was so difficult and all I wanted was to rest. I needed relief from the fear and pain I had been living in for months. Then, I realized that I didn't want to die like that. Not then. I reminded myself that I needed to be strong and find a way to breathe. I struggled to gulp down the air I needed to fill my lungs, praying to God with each effort to breathe. I don't know how much time passed like that, but eventually, I was able to start breathing and they quickly put on a noninvasive ventilation mask until my surgery.

The boys were now old enough to know how serious my condition was, and it took a toll on them. For the first time, they saw everything I was going through, and it put a heavy amount of stress on them. Isaiah especially. I got a call from his teacher who said that he was misbehaving in class. When she pulled him aside to ask him what was wrong, he told her I was in the hospital.

When she called me, she was concerned for all of us. I could hear the worry in her voice, and I wondered what she thought was going on. I told her about my condition and what was going on surgery-wise and how much stress had been on all of us. She seemed relieved that no one was in danger, promised to watch out for Isaiah, and wished me luck for my upcoming surgery.

Finally, the day I had been fighting to stay alive for came. My mother stayed with me in the room for as long as she could. She held my hands and prayed over me, claiming the protection and provision of the Lord over me and my team of doctors. As I watched the overhead lights flash by on the gurney ride to the elevator, I felt peace like a river cover my soul. I knew that God would do everything according to His will, whether I lived or died. When I entered the room, I prayed and gave God credit for the miracle that only He could perform in that operating room. I said, "God, I know you're already present in this room…I'm going on that operating table alive and I'm getting off of it alive and I believe everything will go well by your grace."

I could feel His presence brush against me as the anesthesiologist put me under, and I knew without a doubt that God would heal my body. When I woke up from the surgery, I had a PICC line in my left arm, a bladder catheter, two chest tubes, three pacing wires leading to my heart, and I was intubated. I didn't know it was possible to have that many things coming out of my body at once, but I realized that God had once again saved my life.

With each miracle He performed, each answered prayer, I understood how deeply God cherished me and how much He provides for us as His children. I felt less nervous when I had my third surgery because I knew that the words of Hebrews 13:5 were true: "For He has said, 'I will never leave you or forsake you.'" I repeated this truth to myself as I took short walks around the Cardiovascular ICU. I would walk around the unit for maybe thirty seconds. I felt proud to be able to and was excited to eat solid foods again (I got tired of the tasteless post-op liquid diet I was on). I also had to practice deep breathing and coughing at regular intervals, to help keep my lungs clear of another Pneumonia infection.

I progressed day by day until finally, my team agreed that I was ready to be discharged. Nine days after surgery, I still had a little bit of fluid around my lungs, but my doctors agreed that if I continued to walk as much as I had been in the ICU hallways, that I could get rid of the excess fluid and prevent Pneumonia. Finally, I could go home. Once I was discharged, I continued to see Dr. Alvarez on a regular basis to treat the Pulmonary hypertension in my lungs. Now I have to continue taking care of myself at home. It's a bit of an adjustment, to go from your normal routine to readjusting to the simplest of everyday activities after heart surgery, but it's worthwhile and can be done.

My new bioprosthetic valve fits perfectly and remains in place. My lungs are treated and clear. I am now enjoying life, my children, family, and loved ones. I'm the healthiest I've been in years, and I could not be more grateful for my new lease on life. I was lucky to have gotten the surgery when I did, because COVID-19 hit heavy the following year, and my appointments were pushed back by six months. Had I been in that fragile state just less than a year later, my story might have ended very differently. But it didn't. God is good, and in fact, my last two checkups had the best possible outcome.

I saw my Cardiologist first, and he said I could stop taking the lung medication, so I did. He told me that my lungs were healthy, and that he wouldn't need to see me for another year. Then I saw my Pulmonologist , and he asked if I was still taking the medicine.

"I'm not."

"You're not taking it? Why not?" he asked.

"Because I saw the Cardiologist and he said that I didn't need it anymore, so I weaned myself off of it."

"That's good." he grinned. "Because I was going to tell you that you didn't need it anymore. You're doing really well, Carline. And now you don't have to see me for another year or so. We're here if you need anything, but as far as I'm concerned, you're good to go."

*Carline's first Sunday back in church,
just four months after heart surgery*

Years of struggle and worry and sickness have finally come to an end. I am heading toward my healing journey and I am doing well. I will still exercise, and yes, I will still stick to my heart healthy diet (even though I occasionally cheat). I will make sure I stay healthy, but that part of my life is over. I'm thrilled to be able to focus all my attention on my family, my boys, my businesses, and my graduate studies. I'm doing everything and I'm loving it. I study and work all night long, and spend the day with my family.

This isn't the end of my story, but it is the end of *that* part of my story.

# CONCLUSION

Being a single mother is not fun. It's very challenging. It's so hard to juggle everything while also being attentive to your children. No one is helping you. You're all by yourself trying to do everything and hoping that it's enough. You have to be the mom and the dad. You have to be the nurturer and the disciplinarian. You have to be fun and trusting and kind while also keeping an eye on their school work and instilling morals and religion while preparing your children to be ready for the world. But if you have to do it by yourself, you can.

Enjoy the little moments. Kids grow up so fast. One moment they're this tiny little bundle, and the next they're studying for the ACT. You'll ask yourself where the time went. Didn't you give birth to two babies not too long ago?

It's easy for single mothers not to prioritize their kids. It's hard not to get caught up in your own emotional needs and wants. Sometimes it's best to remain single and focus on yourself and your kids. Prioritize your little family. Don't jump from relationship to relationship. Don't introduce them to the negativity and toxic habits of bad relationships.

Don't lose hope. Bad things happen to good people, and it's not your fault that you're single. Work hard. Trust God. Don't give up. Things will get better. They will.

I'm going on eight years of being single, and it's hard. I've never been the type of girl to jump from man to man, and I thank God for that. I thank God that my parents were strict and raised us to respect and honor ourselves. They were stern, but it helped shape the way I look at the world. It's more than just "staying single," it's about protecting your kids from a potential harmful relationship. Can you focus on giving your kids everything they need during such a crucial time in their lives if you're focused on going out and dating?

I'm sure there are women who can, but I truly believe that things happen when they're meant to happen. You won't meet your Mr. Right until the *time* is right. No amount of worrying and stressing is going to make it happen sooner. Take that time you would have been spending dating and going out, and redirect it to focus on your children's wellbeing. Don't get distracted. Things do get easier.

To tell the truth, I'm ready. I'm just as ready for that next chapter as anyone, and my children are, too. They're ready for that father figure. They're ready to have someone teach them how to be men. They need to have someone in their lives that can teach them all the things I can't. We waited, and now they're ready for our family to grow and expand. They pray that the Lord will bring someone into our lives, and it warms my heart. I'm so glad I waited for them to be ready for that change in their own time. I wanted them to feel comfortable. I didn't want to push them into something they weren't ready for.

My kids are happy. They're learning and coming into their own. They're doing well in school and push themselves everyday to do better. I'm proud of myself and I'm proud of my boys. We've made good use of our time and have worked on our shortcomings. We've focused on our family and on ourselves as individuals. We've grown and achieved so much over the past eight years, and when the time is right, God will bring us to that next chapter in our lives, and it will happen in His timing.

I've had to learn and relearn many things in my life. I've had to learn how to forgive and keep on forgiving. Storms are inevitable in life, but they vary through time and seasons. Everyone is bound to face one storm or another when passing through the journey of life. When we are faced with challenges, we should face it because it's just for a moment; and it will surely pass. Our challenges do not determine who we are, but *where* we are. We should be focused; this storm will surely pass.

Our focus should not be on our pains, but on our dreams. Every situation is meant to bring out the best in us. We are to learn through those storms of life that there is always a reason for them, sometimes they are **blessings in disguise.**

We are more than conquerors. Keep your faith, and pray.

# THERE IS ALWAYS HOPE

I am a witness of our Lord's love and healing power. I feel strongly that people should not give up— God did not give up on me, even though things looked bad, and that is so important. I no doubt have seen many miraculous things happen in my body and I thank God for every doctor, nurse, and specialist who took care of me and my babies. I strongly believe and have definitely acknowledged the hand of the Lord in my life.

I am believing that in the days ahead, many people will rejoice at what the Lord has done and even catch a wave of God's salvation for themselves. I want you to know that the fear of the Lord is the beginning of knowledge (Proverbs 1:7). I am grateful that we are alive and I thank God each day for His grace, mercy, and favor toward my family. Our energy persists beyond death, even if our physical body does not. Energy is neither created nor destroyed. For me, this is an understanding rather than a feeling.

I encourage each person reading this book to never give up. As long as you are alive, anything is possible. Remember that you are stronger than you think. Don't compare yourself or your situation to others. It will cause you to regret what you were never intended to be, instead of allowing you to enjoy how God uniquely created you. Comparing ourselves and our situations to others will always rob us of gratitude, love, joy, and fulfillment. It prevents us from fully living our lives. I pray my journey will bring others hope and healing.

My journey has been quite a roller coaster ride. What has helped me get through it all is the support I've found through family and friends, and most importantly, reading God's word and having a close relationship with Him. For as long as I can remember, my mother made sure I understood that God is like no other, and He has saved my life. My mother also told me she would pray that I would not only know Jesus as my savior, but that I would live out that love in kind, compassionate, and tangible ways. The doctors told me that it would only be a matter of time before I would become a statistic.

But I am not a statistic.

I am a miracle.

A survivor.

A believer.

I am a strong and courageous woman who God has equipped with a mission for my time here on Earth.

Just like you.

# A POEM FOR MY BOYS

*To my sweet boys Gecarr & Isaiah,*

*Long before God laid Earth's foundations, He had you in mind.*
*You were conceived in the mind of God before you made your entrance in this world.*
*Thank you for answering the call of God for your life to be here.*
*It is not fate, nor chance, nor luck, nor coincidence that you are breathing at this very moment.*
*It is because God has a grandeur plan for your life.*

*I can testify that you've turned out to be more than I ever imagined.*
*You're more than what I prayed for.*

*You're the best sons a mother could ever ask for.*
*You are my joy and my pride, a tool in God's hands, a*
*headache to my enemies, and a gift to this world.*

*Thank you for being so loving, so caring, so kind, so*
*generous, so respectful and so sensitive to the Spirit of God.*
*You are an absolute pleasure to watch as you bring the*
*harvest in with class, dignity, wisdom and understanding*
*beyond your years.*

*My baby boys,*
*Don't let anyone bring you down without your consent.*
*I wish I could promise you that life will be easy, but I cannot.*
*However, I can promise you that it will be better and brighter*
*as long as you choose it to be.*
*Your race and nationality are no accident, therefore don't pull*
*back, no, don't shy away.*
*Look life straight in the eyes as you intentionally march*
*toward destiny with dignity and honor and your head high*
*with pride,*
*your shoulders square with strength and your heart loaded*
*with the love and the fear of God.*

*You were born to fulfill something on this Earth.*
*Go for it with everything in you.*
*Fight with every breath in your lungs and all the strength in*
*your body to stand out because you were not born to fit in.*

*You are great powerful leaders, yes, that's exactly what you are!*
*I believe in you and I believe in the God who shines in you, through you, around you for His glory.*
*I urge you to be the men God created you to be.*

*I know deep within my soul you will make me proud.*
*I pray you make the right decisions in everything you do.*
*I pray for your future wives.*
*I pray and bless your children and their children.*
*I pray that you receive more wisdom, understanding, power, knowledge, counsel, strength, and fear of God as you continue on your life journey.*
*I made a covenant with God that you and your descendants, till the generation when Jesus Christ comes back to earth, belong to Him forever.*

*May these words echo in your soul when I'm no longer here to speak to you.*
*Know that you're the best thing that could ever happen to me both in this life and the life to come.*
*Gecarr and Isaiah, I, Carline Edouard, your mommy, loves you with all my life!*

Gecarr (3) and Isaiah (2) in 2008

## CARLINE EDOUARD PERSONAL COLLECTION

*Carline, Gecarr (left), Isaiah (right) and
Whitney (niece)*

Christmas in Texas

Texas Christmas in the new family
apartment

Christmas pictures

Carline's Mom with baby Gecarr

Gecarr, Carline, Isaiah and her Dad, Winston, in Texas,
March 2018

## About the Author

Carline lives in Miami, Florida, with her teenage sons, Gecarr and Isaiah. A true business woman, Carline is currently building her businesses while studying for her Master's degree. Carline is writing several new titles, and will release them later this year.

Made in the USA
Columbia, SC
17 April 2021